Further praise for *Ci*

'This is a book for our time. An illuminating, coherent and gripping story of what we are living through, with a hopeful ending.'

Mary Kaldor, founding member of
European Nuclear Disarmament and
the Helsinki Citizens' Assembly

'Sharp, short and unshackled, Marsili and Milanese show that if the EU is ever to become a genuine democracy, it will be because ordinary citizens have understood that we need a refresher course in the practice of liberté, egalité, and fraternité, and are coming together everywhere to ensure it.'

Susan George, author of *Shadow Sovereigns* and
Whose Crisis, Whose Future?

About the authors

Lorenzo Marsili has degrees in philosophy and sinology. He is the co-founder of European Alternatives, one of the initiators of the pan-European movement DiEM25, and founding editor of the independent quarterly journal *Naked Punch Review*.

Niccolò Milanese is a poet and philosopher and co-founder of European Alternatives. He has been involved in the founding of numerous political and cultural organisations, magazines and initiatives on several sides of the Mediterranean.

Citizens of Nowhere

How Europe Can Be Saved from Itself

Lorenzo Marsili and
Niccolò Milanese

ZED

Citizens of Nowhere: How Europe Can Be Saved from Itself was first published in 2018 by Zed Books Ltd, The Foundry, 17 Oval Way, London SE11 5RR, UK.

www.zedbooks.net

Typeset in Adobe Caslon Pro and Haarlemmer
by Swales & Willis Ltd, Exeter, Devon
Cover design by Clare Turner

A catalogue record for this book is available from the British Library

ISBN 978-1-78699-369-4 pb
ISBN 978-1-78699-371-7 pdf
ISBN 978-1-78699-372-4 epub
ISBN 978-1-78699-373-1 mobi

Printed and bound by CPI Group (UK) Ltd, Croydon, CR0 4YY

Contents

Foreword by Tania Bruguera   xi

Introduction: Citizens of Nowhere   1
  News from nowhere   3
  What is Europe the name of?   6
  Time travel, eternal returns and other utopias   8
  European alterities   13

1 Broken Clocks   19
  The Greek spring   19
  A Chinese encounter   23
  Is it the economy, stupid?   27
  No, you can't   30
  A revolution from above   33
  The story of the two Europes   35
  A cure for impotence?   40
  Interregnum   41
  Underlying symptoms   44
  Enter depression   49
  All change   50
  Clocks of land and clocks of sea   52

2   The Wizard of Oz   55
    The mechanical Turk   55
    The birth of the disembedded market   57
    The return of the illusion of natural markets   59
    Market machine gun   61
    The double movement   64
    Who does a home belong to?   66
    No state is an island   72
    Stop the ride, we want to get off   81
    The European archipelago   84
    We are the lions, Mr Manager   91
    Striking a light   97
    We don't want your charity   101
    Putting out the lights   102
    The pirate federation   105
    Europe as metaphor for the world to come   109

3   If Europe Is a Fortress We Are All in Prison   118
    Face to face with the unbearable inequality
      of free movement   118
    Schizophrenia   121
    The official European response: a denial of
      reality   126
    The best hotel in Europe   129
    Open access   132
    The rights of man and of the citizen   136
    First they came for the Roma   149
    Citizenship out of the prison   153

Contents

4 Beyond Internationalism: A Transnational
       Interdependence Party   159
    The power of nobody   159
    Nationalism and internationalism   162
    The International   165
    Beyond anarchy, state and class   173
    Of forums social and unsocial   175
    The world's colony   180
    A party with a new worldview   184
    Who does the party belong to?   189
    A party beyond and between the institutions   194
    Starting in Europe   206

Citizens of Nowhere: A Rallying Cry   213

Afterword by Yanis Varoufakis   217
Notes   223
Bibliography and Further Reading   241
Index   247

Foreword by Tania Bruguera

'We have been called many names. Illegals. Aliens. Guest workers. Border crossers. Undesirables. Exiles. Criminals. Non-citizens. Terrorists. Thieves. Foreigners. Invaders. Undocumented.'

This is the beginning of the Immigrant Movement International Manifesto, that I read outside the Saint Bernard Church in Paris during the Transeuropa Festival of European Alternatives in 2012. That church is famous as a historical centre of the *sans papiers* movement. This book tells some of the stories of the ways in which we have all had our rights devalued under a regime of nationalism and neoliberalism in which migrants – and very often female migrants in particular – are in the front line: both suffering the effects, but also leading the fight back and the alternatives.

There was a moment when Europe played with hope; it was when we heard of Schengen Visas and Pirate Party, of a unified currency and Iceland asking the banks and not its citizens to pay back for their mistakes. Today, when Europe has forgotten its own story of nationalisms, economic corruption and the consequences of its poor treatment of immigrants, the 'hope exercise' seems like an old fairytale.

The moment of popular participation has transformed into populism and politics has become a cynical practice few see as legitimate. Political hope comes out of a combination of a re-imagined collectivity and proposing new avenues to access power. This is what people are doing, taking the political instead of politics into their hands, and this is what organisations such as European Alternatives (with the plurality of its 's' at the end) are bringing back to us: our power through a transnational creative political force.

In May 2015 I organised a public reading of Hannah Arendt's *The Origins of Totalitarianism* in Havana. That year European Alternatives organised public readings of the book across Europe, along with other organisations throughout the world. The readings were a collective act of solidarity with the citizens of Cuba, whose democratic rights are systematically denied, but it became a symbol of the growing misuse of democracy with all those artists, journalists and activists imprisoned everywhere, and also a reflection and a protest about the plight of refugees in Europe, the nation state system and growing authoritarianism throughout the world. Political gestures are the language of those with no power – from filling the squares with discontented bodies to creating alternative institutions. Today artivism (art and activism) is a joint practice giving spaces of self-expression to people who want to send a message to those in power. Political actions are not a formal practice; they are informed with what I call *Political-Timing Specificity*, which is the understanding of the agency you have as a citizen, and the timing of your demands and observations at the moment when those decisions are being taken and not after the fact. It is the way for citizens to step into the doors of the building that belongs to them and not to those who try to silence them.

Here is a book on the frontiers of political invention, calling for new forms of solidarity, new institutions and new parties that go beyond borders. It shows us it is not enough to resist, but that we must enter into places of power and reinvent them, whether they are art galleries or parliaments. Here is a book which talks of Europe but of everywhere else as well, which questions any idea of centre or periphery.

Here is a book for reading yourself or together with others, for reading in different places at different times, in public, in private. And through this reading we can find a force to speak and act and invent our own names.

This book will invite you to transform your social, economic and political discontent into political effectiveness. Today the political is in the hands of the people; it is in your hands.

Introduction

Citizens of Nowhere

> If you believe you are a citizen of the world, you are
> a citizen of nowhere. You don't understand what the
> very word 'citizenship' means.

Theresa May made these comments in the closing
address to her first Conservative Party conference as
Prime Minister in October 2016. It was a speech in which
she tried to distance herself from Margaret Thatcher's
(in)famous phrase 'there is no such thing as society',
instead emphasising the 'bonds and obligations that make
our society work' and attacking tax-dodging companies
and celebrities, as well as unscrupulous big-business directors who do not train up or care for their staff. This was the
speech in which she attempted to set out her 'philosophy'
and 'vision' for Britain following the Brexit vote in June: a
vision of 'a country that truly works for everyone, not just
the privileged few', in which an interventionist government
steps in to correct injustice, ensure equitable distribution
and opportunities, and end a regime of one rule for the rich

and another for the poor. Just as she had been doing since becoming leader in July, she was attempting to steal the clothes of the Labour Party by defining the Conservatives as the party of workers' rights, the party of the NHS, the party of constructing houses, the party of social justice.

The underlying nationalism of Theresa May's message, which drew from the Leave campaign's often openly xenophobic stance, has sadly not evaporated in UK political discourse – unlike her authority or credibility. Instead, it has become more entrenched as the Brexit process moves forward. The division May draws between deterritorialised elites who escape all social obligations and 'everyday' local people who pay their fair share of taxes is equated with the distinction between those 'out-of-touch' 'traitors', 'mutineers' and 'enemies of the people' who call into question the good sense of Brexit and those 'patriots' who enthusiastically cheer it.

Brexit is, of course, a story unique to the United Kingdom, but the right-wing discourse of a turn against 'global' elites – constantly mixed up with migrants, left-wingers and human rights – is a common one throughout the Western world. Always ready to shift their arguments to maintain privileged positions, many voices of the establishment pronounce in grave voices that perhaps elites have raced too far ahead in a process called 'globalisation', leaving poor citizens unable to catch up. The teacher should slow down for the dim ones at the back! Faced with rebellion, now is the time to calm everyone down, to return to the nation, to return to the territory and forgotten populations. Or so the story goes. We think this story is quite wrong, perhaps because we have more belief in – and probably more familiarity with – citizens than those forging the mainstream narratives. And in this book we will seek to overturn this dominant discourse.

While May's national populism is regressive and often racist, there is a way of *misreading* her phrase on citizenship that perhaps reveals its deeper truth and hidden energy. For what if *we are all* citizens of the world, and *for this very reason* we are citizens of nowhere? This sounds like a paradox, which is a sign that it works against prevailing common sense. But it is precisely by undermining ideological common sense that we can unpick the nationalist strategy, at once recovering a radical dimension to citizenship, creating a post-national horizon of political action, and providing a way to re-contextualise widespread feelings of disempowerment. As we describe in Chapter 1 of the book, the only way to offer genuine political alternatives is to reframe the problem. We will show that the nation is no longer a sufficient vehicle for progressive civic engagement, and that a radical reinvention is required to redirect the course of global politics.

News from nowhere

There is no reason to follow May in consecrating tax dodgers and brutal capitalists as 'cosmopolitans' rather than calling them simply 'criminals' or 'exploiters' and actually doing something about them. Instead, we contend that it is ordinary folk who have become citizens of the world. In contemporary Europe, and increasingly across the globe, very many of us – who are by no means economic elites – have access to information from throughout the world, the possibility to communicate with faraway places, and the opportunity to travel reasonably cheaply. In a globalised economy – and especially since the 9/11 terrorist attacks and the 2008 financial crash – it is clear that we can all be affected dramatically by events elsewhere in the world. Furthermore, we already know that climate change is damaging societies and lives. Whereas in earlier centuries only tiny elites may have been 'citizens of the world', now the world is more open to the masses than ever before, and the millennial generation has grown up taking this increased awareness for granted.

And yet if we understand citizenship as having the political agency to influence the course of our collective future, we indeed lack a citizenship of the world: only very few people have real agency regarding our future, and while some have more rights and privileges than others (votes in more or less powerful countries, greater social and economic capital and mobility), the vast majority of us are 'citizens of nowhere' to some extent, and we will remain so until we invent political forms of agency that are equal to the forces which shape our world. So we have simultaneously 'gained' the world in our awareness, and 'lost' the world under our control.

This inverse relationship is expressed in particular in opinion polls of young people. Many recent polls have shown that younger generations see themselves in global terms, with a wide range of responsibilities to people both close and distant from them.[1] There are generational shifts in many parts of the world when it comes to seeing community as defined in civic terms rather than based on ethnicity, family ties, religion or territory. And yet younger generations also say that they feel excluded from society, and disempowered, particularly in countries that have experienced recent economic crises.[2] These two sentiments both go together and are in tension with each other: increased horizons go hand in hand with a feeling of powerlessness and exclusion, and that impression is increased if one feels that unchallengeable global events are driving local economic and social problems.

Thus, it is too simple as well as patronising to argue that elites have raced ahead in globalisation. A significant part of the population is more globally aware than the elites give them credit for, and precisely because of this awareness of what is going on they find the current course of politics infuriatingly wrong: wrong in its objectives, wrong in its results, and wrong in its methods. What is more, as we will show, citizens are ready to act to change the course of history, but where the political establishment has not attempted to stamp out these energies for change (and that has happened very often), then unresponsive, unimaginative and out-of-date institutions and ways of thinking have stifled new initiatives.

The key slogan of the Brexit campaign was 'Take Back Control'. There is no possibility of being able to completely *control* the future, and the backwards-looking nostalgia of this phrase is to be rejected. However, the demand for citizens collectively to decide their future is fully justified. Where the Brexit campaign and the rhetoric of the May government were duplicitous was in promising that this meaningful citizenship could be found in the nation. As we argue in Chapter 2, the global neoliberal economy in fact relies on the mirage of national sovereignty to hide its real operation. And so to 'take back control' we must not recoil into the bosom of the nation, but step beyond it.

What is Europe the name of?

Before Europe was a geographical space it was a myth: the myth of the goddess Europa abducted by Zeus, who disguised himself as a bull and carried the beautiful Europa away. As the myth is told by Apollodorus, Europa was the daughter of Agenor and Telephassa and had three brothers: Cadmus, Phoenix and Cilix. After her abduction, Agenor sent the three brothers to find Europa, telling them not to return until they had done so. The brothers set out in three different directions: one heading towards what today we would call Europe, one towards the Middle East, and one towards Africa.

At a time when many would like to define Europe along ethnic or national lines, and at a time when the proliferation of border fences goes hand in hand with the identification of an indigenous 'people', the story of Europa serves to remind us that from the beginning 'Europe' has been thought of as bigger than it is now typically understood as being, and that it exists at the crossroads of multiple paths. Europe, ultimately, is *nowhere*.

Nowhere, of course, is also the etymology of the word 'utopia'. And Europa – just like Utopia – is never found. After a lengthy and apparently fruitless search, the three exhausted brothers established cities in order to rest, regain strength, and continue looking for their sister. Phoenix settled in Phoenicia, which is modern-day Lebanon, Syria, Israel and Palestine; Cilicia settled in Cilicia, which is today's Anatolia; and Cadmus settled in Thrace (now Greece, Bulgaria and Turkey) and founded the city of Thasus, later known as Thebes, a city that would become the very symbol of Greek tragedy. It is a historical contingency – but no coincidence – that movements of people through this part of the world today are leading to another epochal redefinition of the notion of citizenship itself. We will discuss this in Chapter 3.

Europe, then, is not primarily a geographical space: it is a process and a pursuit. Europa does not really exist: she is movement itself. As the Uruguayan writer Eduardo Galeano describes it: 'Utopia is on the horizon. I move two steps closer, it moves two steps further away. I walk another ten steps and the horizon runs ten steps further away. As much as I may walk, I'll never reach it. So what's the point of utopia? The point is this: to keep walking.'

Today, history once again appears to be accelerating forcefully, with all in flux, ebullient. We are in the middle of a profound transformation that will change the basis of our economic model, our democracies, the distribution of wealth and the meaning of words themselves. Disruptive change should not be a novelty for Europe: beyond the myth of Europa, the continent's modern origins rest on a double revolution – French and Industrial – that precipitated an acceleration in time without precedent, a permanent revolution that would be exported to the whole world. Indeed, the very word 'modernity' comes from *modus*, meaning *just now* or the becoming of reality.

The problem we face today is not a *fear* of change, as the elites would have us believe. Rather, it is a justified feeling of losing control over that change, as we face a transformation that our political systems appear increasingly unable to mould and actively govern. Our search lacks direction, the object of our pursuit increasingly blurry. We feel powerless, and our democracies appear a sham. But there is no turning back to the fireplace of Agenor and Telephassa, to a time before our continent and our future were abducted. There is no placing history in a box, renouncing time, hopping off the ride. We need to cross the swamp and continue our pursuit.

Time travel, eternal returns and other utopias

The word 'nostalgia' was created during the seventeenth century from the Greek words *nostos*, meaning 'homecoming', and *algos* meaning 'pain' or 'ache'. Somewhat fittingly, the word itself is a neologism using ancient roots. Although its Homeric overtones conjure up the long homecoming of Odysseus to Ithaca, the word itself is a modern invention. Nostalgia is a selective emotion: different countries had different 'golden ages', and not everyone can easily imagine that they lived like kings. That white, male middle-class Americans have some nostalgia for the 1950s is understandable; it is just as understandable that black, female Americans find the idea of a return to the same era horrifying. Some in Turkey may feel a sense of nostalgia for the greatness of the Ottomans; Christians in Turkey surely will not. Lesbians and gays worldwide may justly fear any nostalgia for earlier periods … unless they go all the way back to Ancient Greece, for example, where homosexuality and bisexuality were the norms. And so on. While some may be nostalgic for a period in which they can imagine they were privileged, others may simply be nostalgic for periods that were calmer or more peaceful, or when things seemed more certain. Between those reminiscing about imagined privileges and those simply dreaming of calmer times, there are plenty of reasons why in our contemporary predicament nostalgia has become a dominant public emotion and time travel a kind of electoral strategy.

This looking backwards has two counter-effects: a constant fear of historical repetition, and the loss of the future. As easy as it is for some to find elements of 'the good old days' in the past, it is much easier to find terrifying examples of where it all went wrong. Fear of a repeat of the 1930s economic slump is a dominant emotion for many, or fear of the 'sleepwalking' that led to the First World War.[3] Anniversary commemorations of the beginning or end of wars have contributed to their heightened presence in public awareness, and for all that these events stand as warnings and can teach us valuable historical lessons, they can also reinforce the idea that disaster is inevitable, generated by forces much more powerful than citizens could ever hope to be. This fear of historical repetition, of eternal return, reinforces the difficulty many of us have in projecting into the future. This is particularly acute for younger generations who are at greater risk of economic precarity, which creates its own difficulties for imagining a happy future.

> 'If I could but see a day of it!' says a man tiredly returning home on a train from a political discussion where different visions of a progressive future have been debated endlessly, and in which he has lost his temper, shouting at the others until the meeting broke up. Arriving home, his thoughts move from the discussion with his friends to a wish for peace and quiet, for bed. Later, when he awakes and leaves his house, he finds society transformed.

This is a summary of the opening sections of *News from Nowhere or an Epoch of Rest*, a novel written by William Morris in 1890.[4] In it, the narrator is transported to London in the early twenty-first century, and takes a journey along the Thames to see a society and a city that have been transformed by socialist revolution, becoming a kind of pastoral utopia in which good fellowship, rest, happiness and beauty are the primary social values. Curiously, the people of this London utopia are ignorant of history in general, and uninterested in anything beyond the forest that surrounds their city: bookish education and adventure and exploration are taken to be all well and good for the small minority who might be naturally inclined to them, but an exhausting distraction from bonhomie for everyone else. These 'citizens of nowhere' are indeed living in an epoch of rest.

Morris wrote *News from Nowhere* in response to the huge success of the novel *Looking Backwards*, written by the American Edward Bellamy in 1888, which imagined a future society in which monopolies have developed into state-run socialist enterprises, society is urban, and the mechanisation of society means that people retire at forty-five and very few do any menial work at all.[5]

Looking back the other way and contrasting these utopias from the late nineteenth century is instructive in helping understand divergent attitudes today. The divisions between urbanite and pastoral ideals, attitudes towards technology, nationalisation, the role of culture, the arts and the meaning of labour are all still present. And yet there is also a sense that we have reached the end of a historical period, and we need to go beyond mourning nostalgically for it and its embedded dreams. We surely have not arrived in utopia, but the time frame imagined by Bellamy, Morris and others has come to a close, and we must look forward into a new world rather than endlessly deferring the expiry date on previous visions: these political utopias have past, their creative energy spent. Going back to their future is impossible. In Chapter 4 we will look at how the organising principles behind the political struggle for these past utopias have also become outdated, and how as a result we need to invent new strategies and scales of action beyond the nation state just as we elaborate new utopias.

Meaningful political citizenship requires the possibility of acting in support of what currently seems impossible. Max Weber concluded his celebrated 'Politics as a Vocation' address in 1919 to the Free Students Union of Bavaria by saying: 'I have to freely admit, and historical experiences throughout the history of the world show, that people cannot be reaching successfully for what is possible, unless one also reaches for the impossible.'[6] We need to be citizens of nowhere in this sense: acting in the name of that which is not yet actual, perhaps not even fully thought-out yet, orienting ourselves to the horizon of our visions of a better society, embracing the divergence of these visions, as did the late nineteenth-century utopians. Directing our vision forward in this way is one of two interconnected preconditions for seeing the signs of a positive future today, and drawing energy and hope from them. It requires not expecting the signs of the new to take the same forms as the old. The other precondition is that we must cut through old narratives which fog our vision: nostalgia is an understandable emotion, but it is frequently manipulated for the political purposes of a powerful few. We need to recover the bravery to break through 'comfortable truths' and common sense.

Introduction

European alterities

For us, the two authors of this book, the journey into contemporary politics started in a prosaic way, albeit in magnificent and evocative surroundings, as we sat down for dinner in Rome in the summer of 2006. Lorenzo, originally from Rome, was back for the summer months from London. Niccolo, originally from London, had been living in Siena, and was in Rome to meet his cousin. Over pasta al dente and red wine, under the darkening Raphael-blue sky, we discussed politics, culture and art, and our sense of frustration at the contemporary situation. We agreed that the nation was simply the wrong political form for any progressive politics that might restore a sense of agency over history for this part of the world. We discussed how, in our view, the utopian idea of Europe had been captured by technicalities, an obsession with rules, administration and economic arguments. It was the year after the referendums in the Netherlands and France that had rejected the so-called 'European Constitution' (which in reality was an unreadable 200-plus pages of mostly technical rules). To use an old phrase from the Marxist theorist Antonio Gramsci, one that became common after the economic crisis, it felt like we were in a period of 'interregnum': as if the old was dead but the new could not yet be born.

By the end of the evening we agreed that simply complaining was not an option. Thus, we decided to organise a series of cultural events, inviting philosophers, poets, artists and others to attempt to recover the utopian dimension of Europe. We settled on London as the most interesting place to launch such an endeavour, for four main reasons. Firstly, we both knew the city well, and indeed it was in London that we had first met a year or so previously through our involvement in several literary magazine projects. Secondly, London has powerful cultural institutions, and we thought that a series of activities in these would perhaps draw attention from others across the continent. Thirdly, London in those years was quite open, and it was possible to launch initiatives without financial capital or family connections in a way that was difficult in other major European cities. And fourthly, and most importantly, London is at once highly cosmopolitan in its population and famously reluctant about its place in Europe: it seemed like an ideal paradox.

Returning to London with next to no money, some slow laptops and a few email addresses, during the autumn of 2006 we created a space for us to work (and sleep) in an officially abandoned warehouse just off Brick Lane, in the East End. Renting from a nearby restaurant owner, we shared the space with some Italian waiters who worked in the restaurant, a Brazilian running something called the London Fight Club upstairs, a carpenter and someone importing parmesan cheese. Opposite was a supermarket selling products targeted at Indians and Bengalis, who are very present in the area, as anyone who has eaten curry on Brick Lane knows. On one of the most cosmopolitan streets in the most cosmopolitan of cities, just metres away from the City of London and yet worlds away from the world of finance, we were in a kind of nowhere space, a place of paradox and contradiction. It felt like an appropriate place to launch our humble attempts at an alternative.

As we started to send emails to potential speakers, knock on the doors of university and museum directors, and ask around to find out who might be interested in helping us, it became clear that we were not the only ones looking for a space in which Europe might be talked about differently. Furthermore, many of these people came from countries further afield than what would geographically be termed 'Europe'. The earliest team included people from France, the UK, Poland, Romania and Italy, but also from Lebanon, Australia and China. The events we put together quickly became something bigger than we had planned, eventually becoming the London Festival of Europe, which took place in March 2007 at the Courtauld Institute of Art, Tate Modern, the LSE and a series of other well-known London institutions. Zygmunt Bauman was the opening speaker, and Vaclav Havel and Jürgen Habermas responded with regret that they could not attend, as did Gordon Brown, who at that time was Chancellor of the Exchequer and told us he was busy preparing the budget.

At the opening event, there were many more people than we expected, notably including people from various embassies and government institutions. They were surprised that there were no reserved seats and some of them had to sit on the stairs. They were even more surprised to see us giving the introduction to the festival rather than some 'official' of one kind or another. 'Europe' was not supposed to be the kind of thing that mere citizens would be active in discussing. We received emails from Eurosceptic members of the European Parliament accusing us of being secretly employed by the European institutions (if only we had been secretly employed by someone – we would have eaten better and had heating!). The Italian national television service, Rai, recorded interviews outside the festival venue. Chinese Central Television and the Canadian Broadcasting Corporation travelled halfway around the world to cover the events. The BBC was not interested ... This is a striking contrast with the contemporary situation, where Brexit and the relationship with the European Union have become a national media obsession in the UK, and a minor news story in the rest of the world.

The success of the festival led us to launch an organisation with the name European Alterities. From the beginning, our interest was in the ways in which Europe acts as a space of encounter between cultures, civilisations and people; and hence 'alterities', 'othernesses', was an expression of our conviction that Europe advances by questioning its own limits and borders – like its founding myth. Once we got started, two things quickly happened: first, we changed our name to the more comprehensible European Alternatives after the twentieth telephone conversation in which we had to spell it out ... and second, people who had attended our events, had worked with us or had heard about our initiative started encouraging us not only to organise the festival, but also to do activities throughout Europe. As early as 2007, it was already apparent that there was a huge vacant space for talking about, promoting and imagining alternative ways of doing European politics and culture, starting with the citizens rather than going over their heads.

When, in 2008, the financial crisis hit the City of London, located just a few hundred metres from our office, that space for alternatives at once enlarged considerably and became intensely politically charged. European Alternatives grew into this space, developing and linking up with other emerging organisations. In retrospect, it is little surprise that no alternative political vision was able to take advantage of the crisis to force the transition to a new world: no alternative political organisation or movement was sufficiently organised or connected across the continent to do so.

But there was also another reason which we think was more crucial: every political movement for change needs a guiding utopia to energise it, but all the utopias to hand were out of date. For one of our early projects we chose the slogan 'Change Utopia', at a time when Obama was campaigning on 'change we can believe in'. Our sense was that 'change' was becoming a major theme of the epoch, almost an empty form of a utopia in itself, because even those promising it were in reality advocating what sounded like more of the same. People were aware that history had not ended, but the collective force to imagine an alternative was lacking. Over the last ten years there have been several *printemps des peuples* with different leading characters and main stages – the Maidan in Kiev (several times),

Mohamed Bouazizi in Sidi Bouzid, Tahrir Square, Occupy Zuccotti Park and Saint Paul's, 15-M in Puerta del Sol, Gezi Park, Syntagma Square, Plenums in Tuzla … Each has had its successes, most have ended in failure, and some are still battling. The story of progressive political change has always been like this. But to a greater extent than ever before, people have been following from a distance, attentive to every sign of change, trying to piece together a bigger picture and foresee the direction of the coming epoch.

Today, looking back at ten years of economic and political crisis, Europe might appear like a continent pulling itself apart: north versus south, east versus west, citizens versus institutions. And yet these years have also shown the hidden vitality and the radical imagination of Europeans acting across borders. While the establishment has been paralysed by lack of vision and ambition, civil society, social movements and many citizens have organised to show that alternatives exist. From the economy to migration, from commons to democracy, citizens have invented new ways of ensuring solidarity and justice; and from these practices, mobilisations and collaborations, a multiplicity of radical ideas and proposals for a desirable European future have emerged. Our experience is that the elements of this alternative are there, living in imaginations, in acts and practices, and they are growing. But seeing them requires a change in mindset, in our understandings of politics and what counts. Through the chapters of this book, we will try to provoke such a change, and propose a strategy for giving these alternatives political force.

Chapter 1

Broken Clocks

If humanity is to have a recognisable future, it cannot
be by prolonging the past or the present. If we try to
build the third millennium on that basis, we shall fail.
And the price of failure, that is to say, the alternative to
a changed society, is darkness.

Eric Hobsbawm, 1994

The Greek spring

In 2015, a small country in the south-east of Europe tried
to appeal to the common interest of Europeans crushed
by years of dysfunctional and unjust politics. The country
was on its knees, social anger at its limits. The middle class
were impoverished, the poor had been made poorer, while
the mafia and kleptocrats were protected by the helping
hand of a captured political class. A proud people were
blamed for the dishonesty of their leaders. With half of the
population not able to find a job, Greeks were derided as
lazy and work-shy.

A small marginal party, with a name as evocative as it is improbable, Syriza – the coalition of the radical left – became the electoral champion of one of the largest popular movements in the recent history of the country. In January 2015, Syriza dramatically swept to power, capturing the front pages of newspapers worldwide, and causing more than one European chancellor to break out in a cold sweat.

The Greek government sought to make one thing as clear as possible: the Greek request was not for contributions to public spending for a bankrupt country. Rather, and more radically, it was for a different solution to economic stagnation, unemployment and the burden of debt for all Europeans. The government requested common solutions to growing public debt, lack of investment in a stagnant economy, zombie banks, and unemployment rates in the double digits. These, it argued, were problems that concerned all of the Union.

Aware of its small size and weakness, the government appealed for support from citizens, parties and movements throughout Europe. The huge civilisational symbolism of Greece was invested in this struggle. The negotiations between the new Greek government and the Eurogroup – the EU's informal but powerful gathering of national finance ministers – dominated the media with an obsessive intensity, as if the future of Europe, and perhaps even the credibility of democracy itself, depended on the fate of Greece.[1] It was not for the first time in European or world history.

In the spring of 2015, Athens became the capital of living European democracy, garnering a world audience. After Tahrir, Puerta del Sol, Zuccotti Park, St Paul's, Gezi Park and Kiev Maidan, massive attention focused on Syntagma Square. European social movements met in Athens, insurgent parties such as Podemos in Spain offered their support, and many young people moved to Greece temporarily to offer material help and engage in a renewed struggle for democracy. We remember well the spiral of meetings, emails, conference calls and international gatherings that went into organising people to support a common demand for change. These acts of solidarity were not just about Greece but harboured the idea that another Europe is possible, and that what happens in Europe has consequences across the planet. The Athens spring focused the energies, hopes and fears of Europeans, whether they were in favour of the Syriza government and its plans or not. And as always at such symbolically charged moments, what happens next – the way things are dealt with by politicians, the media and those in positions of power – is hugely important.

In this case, what happened next was a catastrophe for politics in Europe. It was decided by Europe's elites that the belief in political alternatives was a systemic risk too contagious to be tolerated. It was therefore necessary to impose a harsh lesson on the rebellious and ungrateful Greeks, one that would serve as an example to the ordinary citizens of Europe: the Spanish to begin with, the Italians, the French, and any others who might call into

21

question the economic policies of the Union. Any success for Syriza risked uniting Europeans and destroying the dominant strategy of divide and rule. 'Keep the people docile, make some small technical fixes, and kick the can down the road ...' was the ruling mantra of the elites.

No progressive government in Europe lifted a finger to turn the plight of Syriza into a real contestation over the economic policy of the Union. Tsipras was left isolated at the European Council, forced into a humiliating climbdown after having won a referendum in his country in favour of refusing the deal proposed by the Troika (i.e. the European Commission, the International Monetary Fund (IMF) and the European Central Bank (ECB), jointly responsible for lending 'bailout' money to Greece). European elites used to complain that no one was interested in the European Union, that people were ignorant of European policies, and that they did not get enough space in the newspapers. Now the eyes of the world were on the national leaders, the representatives of the Commission and the ECB, who found nothing better to do than rigidly refuse all questioning of a status quo that was manifestly failing. Given the opportunity to propose a different course for Europe – one of reconciliation, of humanism and decency, and of empowered citizens – the other countries of Europe, the Commission, the ECB and the IMF preferred to dogmatically insist that no negotiation was possible, no better future was available, that everything should simply carry on regardless of the consequences. If a country doesn't like it, there is only one option offered: leave! Thus the Greeks were invited to leave the currency union of the continent they gave the name to if they continued to refuse to submit unquestioningly to its policies.

Several days after that dark night for Europe, Donald Tusk, the president of the European Council, made a series of revealing confessions to the *Financial Times*. Firstly, that negotiations should be blind to all political passions, and purely technocratic: 'negotiations should be about numbers, laws, procedures. The discussion about dignity, humiliation and trust, this is not a negotiation. It is an introduction to fight, always in our history.' Secondly, that in the end he was not concerned so much about the economics, but by the politics and the glimpse of a possible alternative:

> I am really afraid of this ideological or political contagion, not financial contagion, of this Greek crisis … We have something like a new, huge public debate in Europe … It is something like an economic and ideological illusion, that we have the chance to build some alternative to this traditional European economic system. It is not only a Greek phenomenon.[2]

A Chinese encounter

Beijing, late summer 2015. A few weeks have passed since the defeat of Syriza, with Greece forced to sign a new memorandum with its creditors and hold new elections. But despite a crisis that has wiped out 30 per cent of the economy, left over half of the country's youth

23

unemployed, and rendered all of the political parties illegitimate, the Greek parliamentary system remains intact. Widespread protest is followed by an orderly vote at the polls and growing apathy and abstention in the streets.

'All of this would have been unthinkable in China,' says Zhang Ying, a prominent spokesperson of the Chinese Communist Party. 'There is one thing we envy greatly about your democratic system: its resilience. In our country, an economic crisis of such a magnitude and social conflicts of such a scale would have brought about a collapse of the system. And instead you wait for the next elections.'[3]

The long years of European crisis have not passed unobserved. While they have confirmed all the prejudices held by the Chinese elite about the inefficiency and short-termism of democracy, they have also demonstrated its capacity to survive prolonged periods of economic collapse and social discontent.

China's history is indeed based around cyclical changes in ruling dynasties through violent upheavals. But, more generally, the resilience of democratic systems is mostly absent in authoritarian or party-state regimes. These are 'rigid' systems, often incapable of adapting themselves to new circumstances and heavily dependent on 'performance legitimacy' – that is, they are accepted for as long as they deliver. This makes them prone to rupture in cases of systemic crisis, mismanagement of the state, or widespread social and economic malaise. In the Middle East, for instance, the 2011 Arab Spring transformed rapidly into a revolutionary wave precisely due to the incapacity of the political system to direct the demands for change coming from the squares into a framework of non-violent transformation. There is acute awareness of this fact: in calculating the potential costs of a war with Japan over the disputed Pacific islands, the Chinese leadership reasoned that a loss for Japan would have caused a collapse in government, whereas a loss for China would have triggered regime change.[4]

When things turn sour, authoritarian or rigid regimes enter a zone of profound existential risk. The likely reaction is 'stiffening up', pretending that nothing is going on, using coercion and authority to avoid a long overdue change. This can certainly prolong the life of a discredited and unpopular regime, and, in some exceptional cases, provide the starting point for its relaunch,[5] but when change finally arrives – as it no doubt will – it will be disruptive and destructive.

By contrast, the democratic system appears highly 'elastic', able to regulate conflict and give expression to demands for change before they reach breaking point. In a democracy you can replace the *party* without replacing the *state*; and replacing the party should serve to change the way in which the state is run. This is the radicality of democracy: everything is always in flux and contestable. You can declare a revolution through the ballot box. At least in theory.

In the heyday of liberalism many were afraid of democracy precisely for this reason. There is a great body of work describing the profound anxieties of the nineteenth- and early twentieth-century elite that the expansion of suffrage might allow the proletarian masses to take power and overturn the system. It is no coincidence that the story of the extension of the franchise is a long and often violent one, from the Peterloo Massacre of 1819 in the UK to the expansion of universal suffrage only in the first half of the twentieth century across Europe. This was an argument that also resonated, inversely, among the first Marxists, who imagined that a politically emancipated working class could potentially seize power through democratic means and thereby overturn capitalism.

In reality, the opposite happened. Liberal capitalism used the enfranchisement of workers and the majority of peasants to bring revolutionary fervour inside the system and the picket inside the parliaments. It was this *parliamentarisation* of class conflict that provided a mechanism for channelling social unrest, giving birth to a new set of policies which, however incompletely, were able to respond to some of the concerns of the weakest in society.[6] It is no accident that just as suffrage increased in England – i.e. as more and more members of the lower classes were allowed to vote – social legislation accelerated, in good part thanks to a politically enfranchised working class rallying around strong trade unions and the newly formed Labour Party from the year 1900.[7]

Popular rage was channelled and, to an extent, allowed expression in policy making. And so, in countries where this happened – and the UK was a leading example – the explosive effects of the 'black avenging army, germinating slowly in the furrows'[8] were diffused, as the system – and often capitalism – was saved from itself by allowing for profound transformations before the grapes of wrath became the only harvest available to the civic and political order.

And yet, as events since 2015 have shown, this mechanism of democracy, the envy of the world, seems to have broken down.

Is it the economy, stupid?

'Misery acquaints a man with strange bedfellows.' Faced with the proliferation of populist forces on the left and the right, many have implicitly referred to this prophetic expression from Shakespeare's masterpiece *The Tempest*. Or, more prosaically: *it's the austerity, stupid!* This is one of the predominant explanations given in answer to the question of why people voted for Brexit, or Trump, or why 10 million people voted for Le Pen in France, or 12.4 per cent of voters in the 2017 German elections voted for Alternative für Deutschland.

There is much in this explanation which must not be ignored. Across the Western world, as study after study has shown, the middle and lower classes have been squeezed out of prosperity following three decades of wealth redistribution towards the top. Countless texts have been written on the rise of inequalities. The trend hasn't budged since the 2008 crisis; indeed, Donald Trump's electoral victory in 2016 has disproven all those who maintained that the United States, unlike the European Union, had successfully returned to normal.

Yet the signs were there. We might point to the fact that *food stamps*, alimentary assistance for the poorest, almost doubled under Obama's presidency; that the majority of new jobs created in the years that followed the 2007–08 economic crash were those that David Graeber defines as *'bullshit jobs'*[9] – repetitive, badly paid and with little social value; that a large part of these are 'fake' forms of self-employment, such as people who work for home delivery services in the gig economy or Uber drivers who work without any contractual guarantees.[10]

A similar situation can be found in the European Union, where growing inequality and the devaluation of work have generated paradoxical effects such as declining living standards even in conditions of economic growth. We need only think of Germany, which may be the continent's economic powerhouse but it also has one of the highest percentages of working poor in the EU.[11] Or take the United Kingdom, which has the highest level of child malnutrition in Western Europe, with one child out of five suffering food insecurity[12] and 37 per cent of children forecast to be in relative poverty by 2022.[13]

While European unity was supposed to guarantee freedom of movement and the sharing of intelligence and creativity, this freedom is coming to resemble more the forced migrations of the past than the thrilling experience of an Erasmus year abroad. Nearly 100,000, mostly young, Italians abandon their home country each year, causing the country to lose 1 per cent of potential GDP growth annually.[14] Countries such as Latvia and Romania have lost more than 10 per cent of their populations since 2008. The situation is worse on the other side of the EU's border. Over 50 per cent of young people in Serbia look to migrate, prompting the US ambassador to the country to make the sanctimonious but accurate remark: 'It seems to me you mostly export young people. You should find a way to keep them and export other goods more.'[15]

But economic facts are not a sufficient explanation on their own. As many have pointed out, it is not predominately those at the very bottom of the income pyramid who vote for Trump, Brexit, the Front National or Alternative für Deutschland. Instead, the crucial group are those not yet at the bottom, who fear social and economic declassification. And this tells us that psychological and cultural factors are crucial. These people feel the promise of advancement sliding away from them and their children. Pauperisation, social exclusion and labour precarisation, along with a sense of demographic crisis from falling birth rates and increasing outward migration – in short, hard, objective data of decline – trigger equally powerful subjective and psychological effects. Despondency and resentment, social envy, the sense of having been 'left behind' and then derided by the 'winners' of the system, the feeling that anyone apparently 'winning' must be cheating or lying – these are just some of the bitter fruits of longstanding economic decline and the staggering gulf between winners and losers.

Yes, there is much that is true in the view that the rejection of the establishment is a result of years of shambolic

economic policy and the growing exclusion and marginali-
sation of many. Yes, the economy is rigged; and yes, some
of those winning are laughing at the losers. But in recent
elections in Western countries, the people who have the
impression that they are 'losing out' from globalisation
were not the only actors. Popular discontent was instrumentalised by other groups, including a reactionary part of
the middle and upper classes seeking a return to the status
quo ante, and sections of the national and international
elites who seek to increase their power, influence and
profit by upsetting the established order. Economics is not
enough. To really understand what is going on we need to
add another element to the equation: politics.

No, you can't

You are destined for a great Monday! Pity that Sunday
will never end.

It is this line in Franz Kafka's diaries, penned in one of his
regular moments of profound melancholy, that appears
today as the only response that governing elites have
offered to those demanding progressive change. The exit
from the 'tempest' of poverty and exclusion, from a rigged
economy in a rigged democracy, from a scandalous globalisation built upon unspeakable wealth and enduring misery,
continues to represent a Monday that will never arrive.
'Yes, we can!' is a seductive slogan, but many feel what's
offered in place of Monday is an eternal Sunday defined by

the status quo, propped up by repression and masked by cheap cosmetics.

Indeed, if the crisis that erupted in 2007–08 is often compared to the Great Depression of 1929, no similar comparison can be made of the political response offered by Western democracies this time around. The presidency of Barack Obama offers the most significant example. A few days after his first election in 2008, the magazine *Newsweek* wrote candidly that the task for the new president would be nothing less than 'to lead the conceptual counterrevolution against an idea that has dominated the globe since the end of the cold war but is now in the final stages of flaming out: free-market absolutism'.[16] Obama came to power shortly after the financial bubble burst, on the back of an extraordinary wave of public participation and a widespread rejection of 'the system'. With a Senate still under the control of the Democrats and the public image of the economic establishment in pieces, many expected that he would seize the window of opportunity to put forward a real New Deal for the twenty-first century and break with a system in crisis.

But he chose the same old path. He appointed Tim Geithner and Larry Summers to the Treasury, the same individuals who, during the Clinton administration, had enthusiastically removed the last obstacles holding back the financial sector. Among these was the Glass–Steagall legislation, which dated back to Roosevelt's New Deal and prevented financial institutions gambling away the savings of the middle class. Obama's attorney general, Eric

Holder, came from a law firm that specialised in protecting big banks. Instead of fixing the disaster, Obama called for help from the same people who had created it. This was no moral drama of penitence and redemption, but the reproduction of the same financial privileges that had brought the world to the brink of the abyss in the first place. As Tim Geithner put it, the role of the state in those crucial years was to 'foam the runway'[17] for the banks in crisis. The machine had to be rebooted, without any changes to the operating system.

Where the state intervened directly in the real economy – such as in the car industry – this has served little purpose other than to set the same unstable pre-crisis model back on track. Why, as Naomi Klein has pointedly asked, were the bailed-out auto companies not mandated to restructure their business model so as to speed the necessary transition to a low-carbon future?[18]

The 'unconventional' actions taken by Western central banks, such as quantitative easing, have likewise disproportionately benefited the better-off. In the years following the financial crash, central bank purchases have triggered one of the largest increases in share prices since the invention of Wall Street. But given that 90 per cent of financial assets in the US are owned by the richest 10 per cent, the 'wealth effect' this generated was highly unequally spread.

It is as if our politicians have become system junkies: addicted to a highly damaging status quo. When a Harvard survey showed that an absolute majority of millennials were sceptical of capitalism[19] – or, at least, the neoliberal variant they have lived under and seen crashing – Democratic House Speaker Nancy Pelosi responded to a curious young man holding her accountable with this laconic admission of addiction: 'Sorry, we are capitalists, that is just the way it is.'[20] For lack of a genuine and radical proposal of positive change, the powers of reaction too easily win.

A revolution from above

As is so often the case, in its response to the economic crisis the European Union has acted in a way that resists simple classification. On the one hand, it has sought to introduce controls over banks that have led some in the City of London not to be displeased at the idea of the UK leaving the EU. This kind of measure is held up by technocrats as proof that the European Union can act in a crisis. On the other hand, the financial crisis has been exploited to enact punishing, shock doctrine-style concessions from ordinary citizens. Taken as a whole, the European Union response is a mix of 'visible' technocratic initiatives implemented too late in the storm and brutal 'hidden' power politics enacted by the economically strong to preserve their advantages. It can be characterised as a 'revolution from above',[21] carried out mostly behind the scenes of bureaucratic muddling through.

Not only has the continent been unable to move beyond a failed economic ideology, it has been equally unable to reform itself according to the very plans of earlier governing elites. When the euro was first devised in the early

1990s, it was eminently clear to the leaders who signed it into existence that a monetary union without fiscal and political union was doomed to lead to a financial crisis. Precisely that crisis – following a long tradition of incremental integration – was what the early architects of the common currency were banking on in order to proceed to the next level of integration. None of this has happened, and European countries' addiction to the status quo surprises today's radicals as much as it would have surprised the establishment of an earlier generation. After all, former German chancellor Helmut Kohl referred to the actions of his successor Angela Merkel in less than celebratory terms: 'She is destroying my Europe.'[22]

Instead, the crisis has been used by the most powerful to remake the governing institutions of the European Union in a way that perpetuates the emergency, preserving the advantages for certain elites that emerge from it. The excuse given is the lack of consensus from European citizens for further integration, as if consensus were a requirement in changed circumstances to pose relevant questions clearly and make arguments. The longer this unequal, unjust and dishonest set-up is allowed to continue, the more difficult it will become to establish the trust of Europe's citizens in any governmental initiatives, and the less consensus there will be. This is precisely the short-sighted strategy of the strongest in Europe, aimed at preserving their advantages.

For many, the experience of the defeat of Syriza by the Troika and Eurogroup in the summer of 2015 was a watershed moment, where the masks fell off and the power politics of privilege became inescapably clear. The enthusiasm with which so many people had supported the struggle against the politics of austerity and the punishing of the Greek population was replaced by a widespread feeling of melancholy and hopelessness. Many of those who may have been sceptical of Syriza and its plans saw the pretence that the European Union is a rational, post-political, technocratic actor come crashing down. The same applied to the pretence that all countries and citizens are equal inside the EU. Many citizens will have drawn the conclusion that the best protection, in a kind of civil war that dare not speak its name, is to have a strong fighter on their side. That, unfortunately, usually means the far right. All in all, in Greece and elsewhere, the experience of the ten years following the outbreak of the economic crisis has been nothing less than a political trauma, leaving in its wake profound doubts regarding the possibility of changing European policies towards tangible and positive outcomes.

These were exactly the same years when we, the authors, had been travelling across the continent to build up European Alternatives and rally citizens for a different approach. What we saw was a story of institutional timidity above and hidden vitality below.

The story of the two Europes

'Are you a lobbyist?' asked the security guard. 'No, we are citizens, we thought this was our parliament …' 'Then I can't let you in.' This is the revealing exchange we had at the Altiero Spinelli entrance of the European Parliament in Brussels in 2009. During our first activities in 2007, many people had already come to us suggesting that European Alternatives ought to do something about various political issues and outrages: the mistreatment of Roma, the response to the economic crisis, migration policy ... One issue, however, that we felt we knew something about – and where we could see clear action that could be taken – was media concentration in the hands of Silvio Berlusconi in Italy, while he was also prime minister. If the good functioning of democracy in Europe requires having good information coming from a variety of sources, then this seemed to us a dangerous precedent. Somewhat naively, we turned up at the European Parliament with the idea that if such a parliament exists, then surely it should address abuses of power that go against the basis of European democracy.

It turns out that getting into the parliament is not so easy: you either need to be an accredited journalist, a lobbyist, or you need to have been invited by a member of the parliament, who sends an assistant to come and collect you. With a little ingenuity, we managed to get in, and we proceeded to start knocking on doors, explaining to those we spoke to that we felt the parliament should do something about media concentration in Italy. Needless to say, most of the members of parliament were surprised to see us, commenting that they get quite a few corporate lobbyists, but almost no citizens. 'We can't think why that is ...' we replied politely. Some members wanted nothing to do with us, but several said they strongly agreed with us, and would propose a resolution calling on the European Council to suspend the voting powers of Italy in European decision making until the issue of media concentration was addressed. These parliamentarians, several of whom had just been elected in 2009 and were still finding their feet in parliamentary procedures, suggested we draft a version of the resolution, which we duly did (after quickly looking up on the parliament website what a resolution looks like). Of course, some members of the parliament were using us to build an alliance between several political parties – a game we were happy to engage in if it produced a vote for the resolution.

In advance of the vote, the main right-wing party grouping, the European People's Party (EPP), of which Berlusconi's Forza Italia is an important member, attempted to block a parliamentary debate about the situation in Italy (they failed). They also voted against the resolution when it was put to parliament, and, with the help of other right-wing parties and a few confused members nominally from left-wing parties, the vote was tied, which meant it did not pass. The arguments were always the same: the European Union should not interfere in national affairs. But our argument was, firstly, that given the European Council is an important decision maker in the European Union, if there is a serious breach of media pluralism affecting the democracy of any one country, it thereby affects the whole Union; and secondly, if one country is allowed to break the norms of democracy, then other countries will follow suit. On both counts we were proved correct: the cases of Viktor Orbán, the prime minister of Hungary, and of the reactionary Polish government controlled by Jarosław Kaczyński, both of which have taken action against the media, and both of which paralyse European decision making on many issues, show how the sickness spreads. The European Commission is now – belatedly – trying to find ways of sanctioning these countries, though in many ways it is far too late. The EPP continues to protect Orbán, and Orbán protects the Polish government – and in this way key institutions of the EU start to look like a mafia protection racket.

We continued to campaign on media pluralism issues (by running a media pluralism European Citizens Initiative),[23] and meanwhile launched a series of citizens assemblies throughout Europe to discuss issues and ideas of importance to European citizens. By the time of the 2014 European elections, after more than eighty such assemblies in twelve countries over three years, we had a citizens' manifesto full of innovative proposals for addressing the economic, environmental and cultural crisis across Europe.[24] We took this manifesto back across Europe in caravans crossing eighteen different countries, discussing it again with many citizens who expected these European elections to be different: after all, it was six years after the financial crash started … And yet the elections were almost a non-event: uninspiring, parochial campaigns led to the lowest turnout in European parliamentary history.

Of course, the cynics would argue that we should not have been surprised: after all, everyone knows European elections are secondary elections, most people believe the parliament does not have any substantial powers, European Union politics are complicated and distant from people, and so on. We know all this, and we were not surprised. But we do note that there was a serious disconnect between the energy of the citizens we encountered throughout Europe, coming up with proposals, ideas and initiatives, and the uninspired, uninteresting electoral competition of the European elections. With a few small exceptions – such as the breakthrough of Podemos in Spain or the election of a couple of pirate MEPs – the institutions of the European Union appeared entirely unable to connect with the energy of the people. In this scenario, the European Parliament remains open to lobbyists and closed to citizens, while European democracy remains under the influence of big money, fearful of the people it is supposed to represent.

There is indeed a loss of trust in Europe: it was started by the representatives losing trust in the people they are supposed to represent. And there is indeed a multi-speed Europe, as several leading European politicians have been proposing, but it is not the kind they have in mind. Rather, many citizens are ahead in the fast lane, and the institutions are lagging behind, slowed by internal squabbles between member states and the national mindset of most political forces.

A cure for impotence?

After years in which voting seemed to have become an impotent act, charged with symbolism but lacking real agency, for many it is now right-wing populism that has restored weight to the electoral ballot. A vote is now capable, with an election in London or Paris, of making Europe tremble; while in Washington it can make the world shake. Tragically, it seems that it is the far-right populists who have been the first to successfully challenge the mantra of *there is no alternative* and thereby restore an illusion of sovereignty and democracy.

American activist filmmaker Michael Moore famously referred to it as a Molotov cocktail: 'People are upset. They're angry at the system and they see Trump ... as the human Molotov cocktail that they get to toss into the system with Brexit and blow it up, send a message.'[25] But this is more than pure symbolism, more than sending a message to the elites. Trump, the Brexiteers and many of the other forces of the new far right have become the symbols of an *exit* from the eternal Sunday of the governing elites, of an establishment stuck in an eternal standstill and offering nothing but more of the same. The narrative is heroic; as Beppe Grillo, comedian and founder of Italy's Five Star Movement, has put it:

We are the true heroes! Heroes who experiment, who pull together those who fail to adapt and the losers. Because failing is poetry ... it is those who try, with obstinacy, the barbarians, who will bring the world forward. And we are the barbarians! And the real idiots, the populists and demagogues are the journalists and intellectuals entirely enslaved to the regime and the powers that be.[26]

The authoritarian drive can give an illusion of real change to a majority of citizens, and can do so not through 'elastic' democracy but through the muscles of the strong man – from Hungary to the US, from the Philippines to India. It is, paradoxically, a morbid feeling of *empowerment* that can arise from such actions. An authoritarian regime, albeit for a short time, can be experienced as a liberating moment: it often appears to represent the will of the majority, at least at the beginning, until inevitably everyone becomes a lonely, isolated minority.[27] But in the rhapsodic instants of victory, of getting one's own back, it feels like the pendulum is set swinging again. The moment, in the words of Beppe Grillo, when the world is set in forward motion and control over that motion is recuperated. For some, of course, the dream is that the clock is now going backwards.

Interregnum

As mentioned earlier, it has become commonplace to quote Antonio Gramsci in describing the situation in Europe after the financial crisis. We have entered a period of 'interregnum' in which the 'old is dying and the new cannot yet be born'. Gramsci is often misquoted, and so it is as well to give a fuller citation:

> If the ruling class has lost its consensus, i.e. it is no longer 'leading' but only 'dominant', exercising coercive force alone, this means precisely that the great masses have become detached from their traditional ideologies, and no longer believe what they used to believe previously. The crisis consists precisely in the fact that the old is dying and the new cannot be born; and in this interregnum a great variety of morbid symptoms appear ... Meanwhile physical depression will lead in the long run to a widespread scepticism, and a new 'arrangement' will be found.[28]

In words that still resonate today, Antonio Gramsci outlines the parable of an establishment that loses legitimacy among the people and, as a result, becomes a primarily coercive apparatus. Defensively, the main preoccupation of such an elite becomes keeping the emergence of alternative ideologies at bay. Here, it is worth recalling Donald Tusk's words on the Greek spring. And so by hindering the emergence of a credible alternative it promotes feelings of despondency, broad scepticism and de-politicisation in society. This is the time of zombies, when reality begins to morph away from the known past. In the meantime, a new arrangement is found – usually in favour of the elites, if they are smart about it.

There are numerous different moments that mark the beginning of the latest interregnum in European and US politics. There are blows to the establishment that undermine trust and consensus – the protest against the Iraq war, ignored by Tony Blair and George Bush, is clearly one such moment. The time lapse of the financial crisis hitting different countries and different parts of the population provides a series of other such moments: starting in the US with home foreclosures, then in places such as Hungary in the European single market but outside the eurozone, then in the weakest nations of the eurozone – Greece, Ireland, Spain, Italy … The longer-term processes of globalisation, the liberalisation of trade, technological innovation, and the provincialisation of Europe and even the US in the context of the rise of other countries and parts of the world are all connected to this moment of interregnum. Furthermore, the growing rift in the West between those who rule and those who are ruled has joined up with different processes in Eastern Europe, where cynicism in and mistrust of the elite date from before the moments of transition in 1989 (the fall of the Berlin Wall), 1991 (the independence of Ukraine) and 1992 (the breakup of Yugoslavia). In many cases, these countries were promised a return of democracy, but instead experienced the snatching of what was previously public wealth by rapacious elites – or, in the worst case, were consumed by war.

Gramsci's quote is often mistranslated. He talks very precisely of 'morbid symptoms', but the translation often refers to 'the time of monsters'. There is a mystery about where this mistranslation comes from, but it no doubt holds a kind of retrospective appeal given that Gramsci was writing after being imprisoned by the Fascists in Italy, but before the full horrors of Fascism became apparent during the Second World War. Reading Gramsci today, we recall similar ideas that are expressed even earlier in Yeats's 1919 poem 'The Second Coming':

> The best lack all conviction, while the worst
> Are full of passionate intensity.
> …
> And what rough beast, its hour come round at last,
> Slouches towards Bethlehem to be born?[29]

Now we see again what look like monsters and monstrous acts: Trump, Brexit, Orbán's referendums on migration, the building of walls and deployment of troops at borders to keep refugees out. The historical imagination races back and forth between the present day and the early twentieth century, setting off forms of panic unseen in Europe and America for fifty years, often overpowering our capacity to read the new situation attentively. This collapsing of historical time, with the past racing back towards us and the future disappearing, is a profound mark of the end of an epoch, the twilight of a dying world.

Underlying symptoms

The monsters have appeared because of many political failures, including a failure of governing elites to pay attention to the morbid symptoms suggesting the collapse of their authority, and the failure of any progressive forces to replace them. But, above all, the monsters have been produced by the morbid symptoms themselves being put to cynical use by mainstream politicians for short-term political gains. For while ruling elites until recently have often appeared unwilling to compromise economically, they have often yielded in the realm of values and humanity. To take but three examples from the 'Third Way' years: the grouping together of asylum seekers, immigrants, terrorists and criminals was a narrative already being pushed by British Prime Minister Tony Blair when the UK held the presidency of the European Council in 2005. In his 1995 State of the Union address, President Bill Clinton boasted about having 'deported twice as many criminal aliens as ever before', and claimed that these people may have been doing jobs that could otherwise have been filled by American citizens. It was Prime Minister Gordon Brown who came up with the slogan 'British jobs for British workers' in 2009. Neither the Blair, Brown nor Clinton statements are quite as morally bankrupt as those that now emanate from May, Farage or Trump, but they fed the poison that has produced the monsters. The painting of the Third Way years as an era of unrestrained globalisation, migration and the disappearance of nation states is a whitewash that works in favour of the far right.

More recently, Angela Merkel – who at least until the 2017 general election in Germany was held up as the 'leader of the Free World' by some – early on in the Euro-crisis cynically employed the lie that Greeks are lazy, contributing to turning German public opinion against any compromise. Nicolas Sarkozy's speech as president of the French Republic in Grenoble in 2010 highlighted the supposed associations between crime, immigration and the Roma, claiming that the violence Grenoble was experiencing at the time was due to fifty years of insufficiently regulated migration, and proposing that citizenship should be removed from people who committed crimes. The founder of the Front National, Jean-Marie Le Pen, simply responded to the speech by calling for Sarkozy to put into action the words he had pronounced. Indeed, following the speech, Sarkozy launched a vicious programme of destructions of Roma camps and expulsions from France.

As a result of such cynicism from mainstream politicians, the far right has come to dominate European and now American politics. Whereas Syriza may have shown that it is possible to be in government without having any power to govern, the far right has shown that it is possible to be a long way from government but have significant power to redefine what is important, what is acceptable political speech and what are acceptable policy responses. A tiny but well-funded nationalist, far-right, xenophobic group has been able to win the culture wars and shift common standards of decency, but it has only been able to do so due to the lack of moral backbone in mainstream politicians, and, worse, their cynical complicity. Sooner or later, the far right enters into government, and few objections are heard: look at the Austrian elections in 2017, where the entry into government of Strache's far-right Freedom

Party was essentially pre-announced, and the leader of the winning party, Sebastian Kurz from the People's Party, simply adopted the discourse of his rivals to the right.

In the short story 'Deutsches Requiem', written in the aftermath of the Second World War, Jorge Luis Borges recounts the last words of Nazi commander Otto Dietrich as he awaits the firing squad after the Nuremberg trials. Unexpectedly, Otto Dietrich claims victory for Germany. The Allies may have won the war, he argues, but to do so they had to transform themselves into a killing machine as ruthless as the Third Reich. Germany went under, but what it stood for – a new man forged in iron, blood and violence – prevailed and conquered the conquerors. We are thankfully not there yet in Europe, but with his characteristic taste for paradox, Borges provides a chilling reminder that we can lose in victory if we forgo our values and let ourselves become a mirror image of our enemy.

As is usually the case regarding the actions of the establishment over recent years, these policies are both morally reprehensible and practically ineffective. Concessions to the demands of the far right will do nothing to tackle the root causes of support for extremist parties. On the contrary, they will exacerbate them. In the first half of the twentieth century, the pressure of socialist movements led to a number of concessions that revolutionised Western democracies. These were often conceded by liberal or establishment parties, weary of the social fractures that were being created and of the socialist threat following the Russian Revolution. The new social pact achieved the inclusion of large parts of the popular classes in the democratic process (it brought them to capitalism, some revolutionaries argued), and represented a textbook case of inclusion through concession and co-optation. But today, yielding to the demands of the nationalist right will achieve none of that. Requests for shorter working hours, healthcare or social security corresponded to the material needs of the most fragile parts of the population, and addressing those needs provided a valid response to those who felt that they were on the losing side of capitalism. There was, in other words, an equivalence between the material source of social dissatisfaction, the political request that emerged from subaltern classes, and the policy response of the establishment. Today, the causes of democratic disenfranchisement and the social suffering of large parts of our societies have nothing to do with refugees or with Islam. Reducing EU migration will do nothing to make citizens of the British hinterland devastated by de-industrialisation and the precarisation of the labour market better off. Similarly, the threat of taking away citizenship will not address the economic and social apartheid in the *banlieues* in France. Restricting free movement or walling off entire countries simply justifies the false argument that these are the right responses to economic and social insecurity, while doing nothing to address the real causes of the malaise, which have complex economic, social and cultural components. Instead, the result will be constant requests for higher walls and stronger borders. This is a recipe for disaster.

Enter depression

Gramsci indicated that one of the morbid symptoms of a blocked political situation would be physical depression. In 2017, *Scientific American* warned that suicide rates were at a thirty-year high, substance abuse had become an epidemic, and mental health problems were becoming less and less treatable even as treatments for other illnesses and injuries were improving.[30] The European College of Neuropsychopharmacology has said that nearly 40 per cent of the European population suffers from mental illnesses, and that 'mental disorders have become Europe's largest health challenge in the 21st century'.[31] Of course, these statistics are partly due to an ageing population on the one hand, and better identification and diagnosis of symptoms on the other. But there are also signs that the mental health of young people in particular is deteriorating, with the European Commission's 2015 Youth Report suggesting that more young people than ever in Europe are experiencing mental health problems.[32] Faced with a situation of precarity, debt, insecurity for the future, and a blocked political situation, this would be an unsurprising consequence.

This depressed public mood feeds other morbid symptoms, and we have experienced many conversations with young friends who are horrified by the policies and discourses of candidates such as Marine Le Pen, for example, but think that a shock to the system such as the Front National winning the presidency in a major country might be the only way to finally bring about change. In such ways, not only are the desperate led to vote for the brutes by the reactionaries and the racists, but also the depressed and those who have lost all but an apocalyptic hope of a final reckoning with evil fall into the trap. So broken is the trust in traditional mechanisms of representative democracy that nothing short of a system breakdown is deemed a realistic proposition to restart the clock of democracy. Everything has to implode for everything to change.

All change

A young Sicilian prince famously declares in *Il Gattopardo*, 'Everything must change for everything to stay the same.' In the wake of the Italian Risorgimento, this Sicilian aristocrat recognises that to keep his privileges, profound adaptation will be required. This maxim could be taken as the peak of elite consciousness, the ultimate realisation that, unlike other animals, humans have both the power to change their environment and to adapt through changing their ways of life. The crucial strategic political question, then, is who has the greater power to make and adapt to any change. What changes? Who makes that change? Who adapts to the change? The answers to these questions are what make all the difference.

In recent years citizens have had very little agency to make changes, and many of us have weak resources to adapt to the changes that are being driven through: this applies to people just about managing to string together several zero-hour jobs, or to those left deserted by the closure of manufacturing or industrial plants. Plenty has changed, but the change has not been driven by citizens acting politically, and those who have been acting on our behalf have not acted justly in directing that change or even in providing resources for those facing the greatest adaptation costs.

Meanwhile, enormous technological, business, geopolitical, demographic and climate changes have been happening, without citizens being given any sense of agency over these processes, and often being told that politics itself cannot do anything but passively adapt. This is simultaneously a negation of the idea of politics and a political act in and of itself.

At the beginning of this chapter, we argued that the elasticity of democracy resides in the capacity of political struggle and the demands of the weakest to produce real social change in institutions, opening up the possibility of going beyond the failed status quo within the system that is in crisis. Today, however, our democracies are less and less capable of transforming dissensus into coherent political alternatives. They are unable to provide agency over the big changes of our time, transforming our political debate into a parochial and ineffective distraction. Ultimately, our democracies are becoming 'rigid' systems, capable of offering little alternative to the status quo other than their own implosion.[33] The resilience of which Zhang Ying, the Chinese communist official, spoke is disappearing. We ought perhaps to reverse the line of the Sicilian prince: so long has the demand for an alternative been denied expression, that today for everything to change everything just has to stay the same.

The real crisis of our time is a democratic crisis. 'Change we can believe in' was one of the most famous slogans of the Obama campaign. But those promises, in the US as in Europe, have been dashed again and again. Is it still possible to achieve real change without rejecting the system in its entirety? More and more people are coming to believe that it is not. Countless promises of splendid Mondays to come have been wasted without us ever arriving an hour closer. While the clock of history ticks onward, the great clock of Western democracy is jammed.

Clocks of land and clocks of sea

The UK Parliament's Longitude Act of 1714 established prizes for anyone who could invent a way to establish the longitude of ships while at sea. Back in 1707, the Scilly Naval Disaster had seen four Royal Navy ships sunk in dangerous waters after striking the rocks on the Isles of Scilly. The disaster was blamed on the ships not being able to calculate their position accurately in bad weather, and hence a prize was established for an invention that would save ships and lives. Sailors could calculate their latitude by looking at the stars or the sun, but knowing their longitude would require being able to measure time, and the pendulum clock, invented in the mid-seventeenth century, simply would not work at sea. During the first half of the eighteenth century, inventors throughout Europe, notably including the Yorkshire carpenter John Harrison, worked to perfect marine chronometers. A variety of different systems were tested, each one dealing with a different aspect of the problem – one was able to deal best with the rocking, unstable sea, another with temperature changes and humidity, and so on – and the search for ever more perfect timepieces continued into the twentieth century.

The Nobel Prize-winning economist and theorist of artificial intelligence Herbert Simon made an important observation about the history of the invention of the maritime clock: a functioning clock depends not only on its mechanism and substance, but also on its environment.[34] A sundial is of no use in places where there is no sun. A pendulum clock is no use at sea. Simon used this simple observation to define an artefact as an interface between an 'inner' environment of organisation and substance and the 'outer' environment of the surroundings in which it operates.

Similarly, our politics today resembles a clock that has been built for another environment, for another time, and thus it appears to many to have stopped while everything around it is becoming stormy: we fear a crash on the rocks, and we might think about ways of saving either ourselves or 'women and children first' – depending on our temperaments and egotism. To be specific, it is not just our politics but our political institutions and the ways we think about politics that are unsuitable for our times. If we want to navigate successfully, we will have to reinvent them.

Much popular resentment and hope for change focuses either on *policies* or *faces* – the biographies of those in power or of those we wish would replace them. But we think we need to delve deeper if we are to regain agency over the tumultuous world of the years ahead. Questioning our understanding of the *nation*, and fostering a new politics beyond borders, will be at the heart of inventing a new clock for a new environment. This is where we turn now.

Chapter 2

The Wizard of Oz

Modern nationalities are mere artificial devices for the commercial war that we seek to put an end to, and will disappear with it.

William Morris, 1885

The mechanical Turk

In 1769 the ingenious Wolfgang von Kempelen presented Empress Maria Theresa of Austria with a very particular gift: an oriental-looking robot capable of playing chess autonomously. Immediately hailed as a prodigy of modern science – this was, after all, the century of the Enlightenment – the machine was rebranded 'the mechanical Turk' and taken on a world tour. It became so popular that in 1809 Napoleon himself played – and lost – against the robot, while Edgar Allan Poe witnessed a demonstration in Philadelphia and wrote an article attempting to uncover its secrets.

But it was all a hoax. A dwarf was hiding inside the machine and, from inside, thanks to a complex mechanism of mirrors and strings, was able to follow the game and guide its arms. While stopping short of a robotic revolution two centuries before artificial intelligence became the ruling buzzwords, the scam nonetheless symbolises the Enlightenment passion for natural sciences, optics, and the games of illusion that would fill funfairs the world over.

But it also symbolises something else: the hoax that regulates how our economy is sold to us.

It is common nowadays to hear about the need to recover the primacy of *politics* over the *economy*, of democracy over the markets. But this is an illusion – as if markets worked by magic or through some fantastic mechanism of nature! It is an illusion that leads many to believe that there is nothing that can be done in the face of global finance. This is because, so the story goes, financial capitalism has drastically reduced all capacity for reform; it has fragmented the labour movement and frustrated political agency; and it has had so much success in neutralising every agent that could limit it that elections are now unable to influence anything. The clock of democracy is not broken; rather, it has been replaced by the machine of the economy, and we are but its pawns.

The reality, however, is that allowing the economy to act as an autonomous sphere *is itself a political act*, and one that requires ongoing political activity to maintain. Inside a machine that appears to be automatic or magical, politics is hiding and making that machine operate. Just like our dwarf.

The illusion only works thanks to a dual ideology that

at once idealises the market and provides the national prism through which we are conditioned to view politics. The illusion is a particularly convincing one and is hard to dissipate, so accustomed are we to the magical image. We will have to proceed in stages and take on some historical background. Ultimately, though, the economic crisis of the European Union in recent years allows us to see the tricks through which the illusion works, and to suggest ways not to be fooled again.

The birth of the disembedded market

To begin with, it is useful to return to the origins of the market economy itself. In his classic 1944 work *The Great Transformation*, Karl Polanyi, writing about the emergence of free-market liberalism in England in the middle of the nineteenth century, explains that:

> There was nothing natural about laissez-fair; free markets could never have come into being merely by allowing things to take their course. Just as cotton manufactures – the leading free trade industry – were created by the help of protective tariffs, export bounties, and indirect wage subsidies, laissez-faire itself was enforced by the state. The [eighteen] thirties and forties saw not only an outburst of legislation repealing restrictive regulations, but also an enormous increase in the administrative functions of the state, which was now being endowed with a central

bureaucracy able to fulfil the tasks set by the adherents of liberalism.[1]

Liberalism, in other words, was *planned*.

On the one hand, the state had to increasingly turn into a something of a *panopticon* – the disciplinary prison system devised by Jeremy Bentham in the late eighteenth century – to oversee the establishment of a market economy. In multiple ways, in fact, the state had to build an administrative system in which markets could occupy a central place in social life, including relevant contract law, the protection of private property in the form of capital, a currency system and credit markets, systems of wage labour and so on. It had to find ways of dealing with the social backlash and disruptive political action of the groups bearing the cost of the transformation, which led to a significant increase in the surveillance and repressive capacities of the state.

On the other hand, the state had to make sure that the poor ... worked. To do so – especially against a background of mostly peasant workers peculiarly uninterested in abandoning their lands to modestly increase their income in return for a life of slavery in the factories – required draconian new legislation. From the abandonment of the Speenhamland system – a sort of guaranteed basic income for the rural poor – to the removal of remaining restrictions on the buying and selling of land, from the infamous Poor Laws that criminalised poverty to the dismantling of tariffs and subsidies on corn, the state was busy undoing rural protections, introducing the threat of hunger for those reticent to join the new industrial army, and transforming both land and labour into commodities for the new market.

The return of the illusion of natural markets

The history that Polanyi recounts has its parallels in the second explosion of the market, following the 'neoliberal' turn of the 1970s and 1980s. Neoliberalism is a generic name used to refer to a model of economic and monetary policy that sees in the autonomy of the market, the centrality of finance and the state's role as the market's handmaiden the cornerstones of a winning strategy. It is a kind of 'market fundamentalism', as Nobel Prize-winning economist Joseph Stiglitz has called it. Yet the success of neoliberalism depends on a pretence that it is a spontaneous and natural order, an enlightened way for rulers to allow the flourishing of their peoples, and above all not another damaging ideology requiring the coercive powers of the state in order to be maintained. Its chief architect, Friedrich Hayek, appropriated Taoist philosophy to sell his new anti-ideology. At the end of his address on 'The Principles of Social Order' to the Mont Pelerin Society meeting in Tokyo in 1966, Hayek added an epilogue:

> Is this all so very different
> From what Lao-Tzu says
> In his fifty-seventh poem?:

If I keep from meddling with people
They take care of themselves,
If I keep from commanding people,
They behave themselves,
If I keep from imposing on people,
They become themselves.[2]

Hayek's epilogue forms part of a long lineage of Taoist misappropriation. The very term *laissez-faire* was originally adapted from François Quesnay's writings on China, where it served to translate the Chinese Taoist concept 無為 (*wu wei*), a type of purposeful inaction. The basic tenets of Taoism are the virtues of the Three Treasures: compassion, frugality and humility. But despite Hayek's pretences, the treasures of neoliberalism are quite different.

The consequence of this new laissez-faire approach is that the supposed autonomy of the market has to extend to every field – to the labour market, for instance, where it pushes even further the process started in the nineteenth-century formation of the free market economy of turning labour into a commodity. The state needs to act to ensure the necessary flexibility by destroying such protections and guarantees – called rigidities – as may be inherited from the past, and let free competition (among workers) exercise its magic. And so, as the Fordist model of mass production collapsed, the relatively stable and secure work contracts it promoted have been replaced with zero-hours contracts, unpaid internships and extreme flexibility for the employer. Society in general is turned into a competition, in which compassion has little role.

If the market is to dominate the state, it must be given muscle, and capital must be allowed to accumulate in private hands. If in the post-war period the highest tax rate peaked at around 80 per cent for the wealthiest – and to fund New Deal investment it even reached 90 per cent – that figure soon more than halved in many countries. Capital taxation was abandoned, inheritance tax decreased or abolished, while taxes on corporate profits and capital gains were reduced substantially. It is unsurprising that wealth became concentrated in the hands of the very few. There is very little frugality or humility for those at the top.

Market machine gun

Contrary to received wisdom, states have never been more active than in the last thirty years of neoliberal hegemony. Perhaps to an even greater extent than the unrestrained laissez-faire regime of the nineteenth century, neoliberalism is a political construction requiring constant activism on the part of the state. It is a political construction that is deeply anti-political, based as it is on politics strategically limiting the power of representative political institutions and putting them under the dictatorship of the market.[3]

Indeed, that neoliberalism would come to be seen as the withering away of state intervention is deeply paradoxical given its starting point. In 1973, the democratically elected, democratic socialist Chilean government of Salvador Allende was toppled in a military coup led by army strongman Augusto Pinochet. Neoliberal angel Milton Friedman, taking a break from his TV shows, flew to the country shortly thereafter to advise on the economic course of the new regime and cement the influence of his economic ideas. 'Chicago Boys', as Chile's neoliberal adepts had been called, took the helm of the country's financial and economic policy. Market fundamentalism came first under the guise of military rebellion and authoritarian rule.

In 1981, the American president Ronald Reagan did not hesitate to call in military personnel to break an air traffic controllers' strike that was paralysing the country, thereafter ushering in 11,500 layoffs. In 1984–85 it was the turn of the British miners to feel the heavy-handed change of economic paradigm. The conflict between the striking miners and the British government assumed epic proportions, causing two deaths, the loss of 20,000 jobs, the privatisation of many state industries and the disciplining of trade unions in the country.

These were no isolated instances. Over the course of the 1990s, the entire political spectrum embarked on a crusade to free market forces from the remaining hindrances of social justice. The so-called Third Way ushered in a vision of rational modernity suited for a post-ideological and rapidly homogenising, neoliberalising world. Differences between right and left were all but flattened out. It was the first Democratic Party administration to take office after the economic watershed of Ronald Reagan that finally removed all remaining restrictions on financial speculation. In 1999, Bill Clinton repealed the Glass–Steagall Act, which dated back to the time of the New Deal and separated commercial from investment banking, thereby opening the last remaining floodgates to creative finance and ever more abstract speculative products. In Europe the 1990s was a period of social-democratic hegemony, with a majority of countries governed by progressive forces. But they were also the years that enshrined in policy and culture the neoliberal consensus devaluing labour, advancing privatisations and enhancing the rule of the financial markets. It was Tony Blair – and the great academic and policy apparatus that came with New Labour – who trampled over whatever resistance remained in a continental social democracy still nominally attached to Keynesian principles. When Margaret Thatcher was asked what she considered the most important achievement of her government, she is said to have replied 'New Labour'. She was a modest woman, for she could equally have claimed the entire European social-democratic left.

The trend was in no way limited to the countries of the European Community. For countries that had previously been on the other side of the Berlin Wall, the period between the collapse of communist regimes and their entry into the EU in 2004 or 2007 is the so-called period of 'transition' – a neutral-sounding word for what was largely a massive transfer of wealth from the state to private companies and certain predatory private individuals who took advantage of the change. Unlike in the Western countries, where there were still significant social breaks on neoliberal transformation, in the post-Soviet countries the discrediting of the communist system – together with the disarray in which its totalitarianism had left civic and social organisations, and the significant pressure exerted by Western countries to open up markets and make accessible cheap labour forces – meant that the market took over. While the activist hero Václav Havel as president of the Czech Republic was preaching a moral revolution and human rights, the grey zone of bureaucrats, many of whom had simply changed their ideological costume from communism to market fundamentalism, was busy organising the economy on anything but a moral basis. One of those grey-zone bureaucrats, Václav Klaus, later to be Czech president himself, would say in the early 1990s, 'I often feel like I have to teach Westerners how markets really work.'

The double movement

With the financial crash, and the spectacle of governments rushing to rescue the financial sector to the tune of trillions across the US and Europe, the role of politics in keeping the show going suddenly became very evident. After decades of citizens being told that their governments could not intervene in the markets – and, anyway, the resources to do so were not there – suddenly the dwarf had been pulled out of the machine.

As Polanyi already noted, the construction of a new market paradigm does not come without resistance. For each extension of the free market, for each *disembedding* of the market from society, there comes a reaction from those losing out, a countermovement that attempts to reconnect the market to social objectives and protections. Robert Owen, the great British socialist industrialist, put it succinctly with regards to the expansion of manufacturing in nineteenth-century England:

> The general diffusion of manufactures throughout a country generates a new character in its inhabitants; and as this character is formed upon a principle quite unfavourable to individual or general happiness, it will produce the most lamentable and permanent evils, unless its tendency be counteracted by the legislative interference and direction.[4]

As paradoxical as it may sound, if laissez-faire liberalism was planned, social protection was spontaneous. As the state drives painful reforms uprooting communities, precarising lifestyles and leaving people at the mercy of the vagaries of the market, a response kicks in that demands protection and safety. Initially a formless outburst of popular protest, the sentiment gradually channels itself into labour and political representation. And so, following the initial outburst of legislation imposing the market – whatever the cost – the latter part of the nineteenth century saw the gradual introduction of limitations to working hours, basic social security nets and pension schemes from England to Prussia. This dynamic of action–reaction is what lies at the heart of Polanyi's *double movement*, or the interplay between the state-led expansion of the market and the citizen-led expansion of social protection.

In the run-up to the Second World War, following the Wall Street Crash in 1929, Polanyi sees the counter movement expressing itself as communism on the one hand, and National Socialism on the other. In the context of the latest Western financial crisis, we can see a kind of return of the double movement: after the excesses of neoliberalism has come a countermovement of protection, usually from those misleadingly called 'populists'. Thus, if we stay within these historical parallels, it can seem like a pendulum is swinging again on the clock of democracy. As we will go on to show, while there is much that is pertinent in this analysis, it misses what is genuinely new in the current situation reconfigured by neoliberalism. But resting within the Polanyian paradigm for a moment longer, we can give two contemporary examples, from Spain and Hungary, to show that this double movement can take very different ideological forms depending on the context and political choices.

Who does a home belong to?

Spain's legislation on evictions is among the harshest in Europe, allowing financial institutions to appropriate the mortgaged home while continuing to demand repayment of the loan from the evicted family. Spain is also one of the countries with the highest number of forced evictions, nearly half a million since the onset of the 2008 crisis – the bitter fruits of a real-estate boom that led Spain to build more houses than Italy, France and Germany combined, and that imploded as the bust saw a quarter of Spaniards lose their jobs.

From 2009, a civil society network, the PAH (Platform for People Affected by Mortgages), started to organise thousands of people in a national campaign against forced evictions and against the greed of banks and financial institutions. The PAH played the role of defender of the rights of the weakest, rights that mainstream politics, including social-democratic politics, no longer appeared interested in. A multifaceted strategy was deployed – from pressure on parliament to civil disobedience, from the presentation of a legislative citizens' initiative with over a million signatures to the famous *escraches*, loud protest events organised in front of the homes of politicians involved in the housing scandal.

The PAH campaigns represent a powerful call for unity between classes and origins: if in other countries the establishment has often managed to redirect popular anger towards the weakest and the poorest – most often migrants and refugees – this operation did not materialise in Spain. The social fracture was reframed as a conflict between an inclusive, heterogeneous society on the one hand – people at risk of unemployment and/or eviction, many of whom were migrants – and a corrupt and oligarchic system based on inequality and financial speculation – the *casta* – on the other.

The PAH spokeswoman, Ada Colau, was often unrestrained in her remarks. 'Organised crime' is how she defined the banking system on a television show, just after having called the Spanish Banking Association representative a 'criminal' during a hearing at the National Parliament. This may sound like harsh talk, but it mirrors an expression used by none other than President Franklin D. Roosevelt while closing his election campaign at Madison Square Garden in 1936: 'We know now,' he said, 'that Government by organised money is just as dangerous as Government by organized mob.'

In her speech, Ada Colau constantly referred to the defence of fundamental rights and to common sense. It was unacceptable that thousands of citizens were being thrown out of their homes and into the hell of unemployment, all the while continuing to be persecuted by banks for repayment of their mortgages, while bankers responsible for the economic disaster were bailed out at public expense and reinstated in their positions. This was a common sense that Spaniards seemed to share: over three-quarters endorsed the PAH's message and disobedience tactics.

In 2015, Ada Colau was elected Mayor of Barcelona on a civic platform based on the actions of the PAH, inaugurating the political cycle that catapulted Spanish municipalities to the forefront of progressive politics in Europe.

Starting from a similar point, things went in a very different direction in Hungary. In the years preceding the 2007–08 financial crisis, Hungary was invaded by a wave of easy mortgages. Most of them were foreign currency loans – in euros or Swiss francs – which were convenient for their low interest rate but exceptionally vulnerable to fluctuations in the exchange rate. At the outbreak of the crisis, the Hungarian forint lost nearly half of its value, thus significantly raising the burden of debt contracted by people most often belonging to the nascent and fragile post-communist middle classes. The number of evictions skyrocketed and protests and social tensions grew. There seemed little alternative to bearing the brunt of widespread social suffering – after all, this is what market principles dictate. A young politician of liberal origins, Viktor Orbán, taking advantage of the Social Democrats' complicity in this system, begged to differ and opportunistically took on the mantle of the defender of the middle and lower classes against cosmopolitan international capital. He won power in 2010 with a campaign based around the defence of those affected by the mortgage crisis, and, once elected prime minister, he immediately passed legislation obliging lenders to convert the foreign currency loans into Hungarian currency, and to do so at a rate established by the government that was significantly lower than market rates. While social democracy was saving the banks and the bankers, the future authoritarian prime minister was among the few to have the courage to clash with financial interests.

In the years following this first stunt, Orbán has undertaken a draconian constitutional reform, has constrained the Constitutional Court, has forced many judges to resign and has replaced them with political allies, has taken control of all the major media outlets in the country, and has forced innumerable NGOs and civil society groups to dissolve, all the while building a clientelist system linking support for the ruling party to the provision of social services and assistance. Simultaneously, Orbán has been stoking anti-migrant, anti-Muslim, anti-Jewish and anti-Roma sentiment, and fabricating conspiracy theories of international threats against Hungary. The young liberal has thus morphed into the primary European advocate of 'illiberal democracy'.

These examples from Spain and Hungary, which could be complemented by many more, suggest that political movement is still possible. The apparent return of the 'double movement', of the call for social protection from heartless free-market capitalism, is indeed important, and the utmost care and attention must be given to directing the countermovement towards social justice and civic inclusiveness and not towards authoritarianism and racism. The state matters, and national politics can indeed still swing – to an extent. The emergence of new progressive parties and movements from the US to the UK shows the possibility of a powerful ideological realignment, one that might exert as much pressure on the centre ground as extreme right and xenophobic forces have done up until now. The discourses on the renationalisation of utilities and the railways, or on fairly dividing the fruits of automation and robotisation, or again on the need for greater fiscal justice and more progressive taxation are just a few examples of shifting common sense in the UK; it is no coincidence that Jeremy Corbyn called his Labour 'the new centre' at a party conference in late 2017.

Nonetheless, it would be wrong to conclude from this that the clock of democracy is up and running again just fine. There are many things that are new in the neoliberalism of the twenty-first century compared with the economic liberalism of the nineteenth, and chief among these is the role, place and unity of the nation state. Specifically, as we will explore in the rest of this chapter, 'the state' becomes fragmented and discontinuous in the context of neoliberal globalisation, and is thereby disarticulated from the nation, but simultaneously we are pushed by neoliberalism to continue to view politics through a national prism.[5] Through this optical illusion at the heart of neoliberalism, the state seems to be both everywhere and nowhere, and we live with the connected illusion that perhaps the nation could pin down this phantom state and make order from disorder. This phantasmagoria of the state and the nation is created by the magic lantern of neoliberalism, and the only way to end the performance is to look behind the projected images and realise that they are ghosts of a past age. In other words, what neoliberalism is and how it works cannot be seen clearly without appreciating the differences in environment, and without an awareness of these differences we will remain trapped by it, or we will labour under the illusion that we can go back to a previous arrangement. Recalling our metaphor of clocks at the end of the last chapter, ultimately a different environment will require a different kind of clock, with a different kind of movement, otherwise we are lost at sea.

No state is an island

The laissez-faire liberalism of the nineteenth century was a consolidation of the empire building that had been going on since at least the seventeenth century; indeed, it was perhaps the crucial element that gave the British Empire an advantage over the others. More important than ruling the waves was establishing markets, from gunboat diplomacy forcing them open – the Opium Wars remain an indelible historical stain on the conscience of any British person – to the clamping down on piracy (while continuing to employ pirates against rival empires, of course). Free-market liberalism emerged hand in hand with a re-composition of the international system and ushered in what is sometimes called the 'first wave' of globalisation (although many scholars see several waves of globalisation prior to this[6]), which reached levels just before the First World War that would not be matched until the opening of the twenty-first century.[7] This extended period of empire building 'outside' the imperial powers also saw the consolidation of the state 'inside' these countries, more or less independently of royalty, depending on the country involved.

The context of neoliberalism's deployment is very different: it comes at the moment of collapse for the post-Second World War order, strategically exploiting the cracks in this international system. It is a serious error to suppose that neoliberalism and globalisation are the same thing: indeed, neoliberalism can only be understood on the basis of seeing its emergence after several waves of globalisation dating back centuries. In this context, it can be seen as the instituting of *global disorder*, albeit a form of disorder transformed by the market from *war* into *economic competition*. And just as the international order becomes disorder, so the internal order of each state is disordered. Whereas free-market liberalism went with the consolidation of the state, neoliberal globalisation goes with the scission of the state into multiple and discontinuous fragments.

Let us look briefly at what came before neoliberalism to better grasp this phenomenon. Following the Second World War, Chicago economist and early neoliberal Jacob Viner wrote: 'there are few free traders in the present day world, no one pays any attention to their views, and no person in authority anywhere advocates free trade'.[8] In the negotiations establishing the Bretton Woods system – the accord that would regulate international trade and monetary policy for the capitalist countries in the post-war period – despite significant differences of interest between the countries negotiating, the guiding imperatives were to avoid economic nationalism and instead promote multilateralism, to facilitate domestic interventionism in order to mitigate social unrest, and to stabilise international currency fluctuations.[9]

At the time, the most internationally famous act of interventionism was the New Deal of Roosevelt in the 1930s, and its success made it impossible to ignore. Of course, a major motivation for all these countries was to prevent their populations sympathising too much with the Soviet alternative and preventing any recurrence of fascism. The boundaries of 'acceptable' democratic politics were set broadly as an oscillation between a right wing that may be more socially conservative and economically liberal, and a left that may be more socially progressive and economically interventionist, institutionalising in the post-war parliamentary regime the dynamic between Polanyi's two movements.

For some thirty years, this system seemed to hold up well: this was the era of state-led capitalism operating under the safe international umbrella of the Bretton Woods agreement. It was a period of regulated global finance and sustained economic expansion, which saw the extension of new social rights – from the welfare state to labour protections – and vibrant national democracies characterised by mass parties, trade unions, social movements and high levels of electoral participation. These appeared to be years marked by the primacy of the political sphere over the economic, with economic policy choices directly impacted by democratic and labour struggles for social justice.

Thus, it is easy to think that our goal today should be reinstating a previous order that the neoliberal interruption has brushed aside. Indeed, there is much nostalgia around a return to the social capitalism of the post-war period: the *trente glorieuses*, when French workers started driving to their factories in brand-new Renaults. And a world order, or at least an economic order, in which it was supposedly clear how the world worked. This picture-postcard view, we should never forget, is highly partial. In the meantime, colonial subjects tried to rebel against oppression and young women tried to rebel against the traditional household. Admittedly, nostalgia for that era is principally limited to certain categories of people in Western Europe and the USA, and with good reason: American philosopher Nancy Fraser, among others, has outlined the often traditionalist, conservative cloak of protection[10] – a mantle that favoured the male, white, Western breadwinner, and that was based on imperial exploitation abroad and patriarchy at home.

Of course, this is not to suggest that this is all that protection can be, nor that the unrestrained free market would have been in any way fairer. But it is important to recognise that the post-war order was heavily dependent on a global division of labour that saw a tiny percentage of the world population thrive and a vast majority survive in persistent, abject misery. While the core developed, the global periphery – or at least the 'Third World' not under Soviet occupation – saw colonial extraction, postcolonial wars, and the odd invasion whenever a leader unpalatable to the 'glorious' West was elected. Once again, it was a certain kind of global arrangement that underpinned Western social market capitalism.

Indeed, since the Second World War, national sovereignty has been little more than a myth if you do not belong to the small clique of highly industrialised countries. True, by the 1970s, colonialism was definitely out of fashion. The Suez Crisis in the 1950s, the long and painful French and Portuguese colonial wars, the extraordinary defeat of the USA in Vietnam by 1975, and a new and widespread national sentiment among formerly colonised peoples – all these combined to make direct military intervention in the affairs of 'developing' countries increasingly unpalatable for Western leadership.

It was precisely in this context that the neoliberal turn took place. Where military intervention – and above all occupation – was both costly and risky, neoliberalism proposed a solution: market discipline. It was around this time that the institutions emerging out of the Bretton Woods agreement originally tasked with maintaining an orderly international financial and monetary regime – principally the International Monetary Fund (IMF) and the World Bank – became highly politicised instruments of international intervention. The so-called 'structural adjustment programmes' plagued developing countries and tested the new neoliberal toolkit on nations too weak to choose otherwise. As African and Asian countries achieved their independence, they found that their finance ministries remained occupied. Markets were opened wide, state properties privatised and rights to the exploitation of natural resources and land put up for sale, in an array of measures that ensured continued dependency on the West and continued extraction of value from the Third World.

As the Bretton Woods system broke down under the cost of wars, the oil shocks of 1973 and 1979, and the Fordist model of production reaching its limits, neoliberalism entered the cracks in the system. It is with the *breakdown of order* that neoliberalism's mix of collective market obedience in the name of individual freedom came to seem an attractive solution as well as a recipe for international intervention. Instead of attempting to define a new global arrangement through discussion, negotiation or concerted action, the task of creating 'spontaneous' order was given over to the market. Like liberalism with imperialism, or the post-war social market economy with the institutions of Bretton Woods, neoliberalism comes to the fore together with a reorganisation of globalisation and the international balance of power. But while empires were fought for and won by militarised states, and while the Bretton Woods system was negotiated and agreed by nation states, the neoliberal system is the deliberate use of the market to create a kind of order from political disorder. The 'order' that is thereby created emerges as profoundly consumerist and depoliticising.

Today, we are witnessing a radicalisation of this neoliberalising process. The very same policies of structural adjustment first put to the test in the so-called developing world have come back full circle to be applied to so-called 'core' countries: the snake has turned against its charmer. The economic and financial system that they themselves concocted seems to be turning against them – or, at the very least, to be treating them with little respect for acquired privilege. Finally, the West is seeing what neoliberalism looks like: think of financial markets mercilessly blackmailing EU states just as they did with the Asian tigers, disastrous structural adjustment programmes being imposed on bailed-out European countries just as they were on African and Latin American nations in the past, multinational corporations breaking any remaining link with their country of origin, or transnational elites hoarding cash in offshore paradises and building bunkers in New Zealand on the off-chance that it all comes crashing down under their greed. The countries of the capitalist core are becoming provincialised, subject to a process of self-colonisation. Suddenly, you can be in the West and sit on the G7 and yet be considered 'periphery', treated with the same predatory nonchalance traditionally reserved for the rest and not the West. Indeed, particularly in the case of European nation states, the distinction between core and periphery has all but lost its meaning. This is why it is a profound mistake to think that the victory of Trump, or Brexit, or even the popularity of a Sanders or Corbyn indicates that neoliberalism is losing its hegemony. Neoliberalism has never been about democratic choice; it is a global system that is not under the control of Western nation states any more.

Indeed, 'global disorder' has become a new buzzword today, with global governance in crisis, G7 and G20 summits reduced to empty theatre, international economic coordination all but failing and the main powers divided on pretty much every issue, from East Asia to the Middle East, from financial regulation to global trade. The unilateral, US-led world that underpinned the introduction of neoliberal globalisation is coming to a close. But as geopolitical turbulence increases, we need to remember that there is no innate contradiction between disorder and neoliberalism. Quite the contrary: it is the *absence* of an internationally agreed political, economic and monetary order that provides the most fertile ground for the primacy of the market and the trampling of democracy. And so, while many rightly celebrate the return of the 'double movement', of the swinging pendulum, in the guise of anti-systemic parties competing at national elections, there is only so much that can be achieved without the ambition of a wider reformulation of our global interdependency and the role of the nation state within it. Ultimately, a new, disruptive economic model requires new international organisation. And today, while European countries and progressive parties see no other option to *this* globalisation or to a return to an irretrievable past, the race to redefine the international order is on.

It is telling that the one country to have fully under-stood this is none other than China. The country is focusing heavily on its internal development, on securing sustainable economic growth and on addressing the stag-gering challenges that a continent state moving from rags to riches throws up – challenges of a far greater magnitude than any European national government would realisti-cally be expected to face. And yet China is deeply involved in a long-term chess game aiming at the reconfigura-tion of Western-designed neoliberal globalisation. At the 2017 World Economic Forum, President Xi Jinping came under the spotlight as a defender of free trade, providing a contrast to Trumpian populism by presenting China as a responsible actor on the global stage. The Belt and Road Initiative, announced in 2013 as a platform for regional multilateral cooperation, links China with regions on the ancient Silk Road, the trade routes through Greater Central Asia and the maritime trade routes connecting East Asia to Africa and Europe. The initiative includes seventy countries in Asia, the Middle East, Africa and Europe, amounting to one-third of global gross domestic product (GDP) and aiming to turn the Eurasian landmass into a strategic alternative to the Euro-Atlantic alliance. Meanwhile, a new Asian Investment Bank has been founded to compete with the IMF and a newly assertive neighbourhood policy is aiming to directly challenge the geopolitical balance in Asia. China has even created the '16+1' grouping of sixteen Eastern European countries plus China, which has an annual summit to discuss Chinese investment in infrastructure projects in the region: over US$15 billion since 2012, according to some estimates.[11] The members of China's leadership are avid history readers.[12] Their reasoning, one that Western progressive parties would do well to adopt, is clear: there is no entrenching of a new 'Chinese model', or indeed of any new model, without an accompanying transformation of the international system to accommodate and nurture it. This is the level of ambition that any genuine transformation of the neoliberal system will require. It is a highly telling reversal of roles that it is now Europe – the continent most obviously associated with imperialism, global ambition and a dynamic attitude to historical change – that seems to have given up any belief in the capacity of politics to transform the world. The result, far from the drive to justice hoped for by postcolonial theory, is parochialism, nationalism and an exclusionary myth of taking back control.

Stop the ride, we want to get off

Neoliberalism can be seen as a kind of market mechanism for creating global order from global disorder, but, as we have suggested with our metaphor of the mechanical Turk, this mechanism is by no means automatic, magic or natural: it requires the constant support of state apparatuses and the action of political decision makers to maintain and advance it. Understanding this might encourage the plausibility of an apparently simple solution: it would suffice simply for the state to no longer support neoliberalism, and for political decision makers to no longer support it, for neoliberalism to disappear! Unfortunately, things are not so simple, and the ongoing chimera of this kind of simple solution is in fact, we suggest, a crucial part of what keeps neoliberalism alive.

The mystification at the heart of this chimera can perhaps best be revealed by asking: 'What *is* the state that would need to withdraw support from neoliberalism?' Neoliberalism is supported by a raft of different kinds of authorities, from central banks to law courts, from trade agreements and arrangements to media power, and to military and security arrangements and agreements. Each of these internationalised authorities reaches into the heart of every state on the planet, and there is no straightforward or neat separation between what is the 'national' state and what is the 'international' set of authorities or governance. Of course, national sovereignty in the sense of control of territory still partly exists, and it would be possible for a nation state to attempt to renationalise various parts of the complex set of governing apparatuses to which it is subject, to renationalise parts of the state. It would be conceivable for a country that is a member of the Eurozone to take back control of its currency, for example, by pulling out of existing arrangements and issuing its own currency. Or a country could pull out of international human rights agreements, or parts of the international commercial code. Or a country could try to nationalise its production and pull out of integrated trans-border supply and production chains. There may be merits in doing some of these things in certain circumstances. But given that each state would remain subject to some of the governance authorities and would need to trade with others, cooperate militarily, rely on international law and so on, the harm to which they would subject themselves by leaving some elements of the international system would surely undermine internal support for pulling out totally. Crucially, this harm is not only, or perhaps even principally, economic: it is a loss of influence in all spheres of international activity, and this would constrain and condition enormously the room for manoeuvre of the remaining rump state. And this does not even take account of the interruption verging on destruction of the lives of all those people in the country whose daily activity crosses borders – economically, emotionally or socially. There is no way to extract individual states from the neoliberal global system: the price of this would be the dismemberment and likely internal combustion of the extracted state. In many different senses, then, 'socialism in one country' has never been a poorer slogan. This is not to say that national levers of power cannot be used more or less progressively; but, as a horizon of emancipatory politics, the nation is a cliff edge.

Another way of thinking about this is to see that the governing political elites are spread between national, international and non-national institutions and authorities. The simplistic class politics of the workers taking control of the state in one country is implausible because it is no longer clear which particular state they should take over (and it never was – Engels and Marx insisted that it would need to be a global revolution; see our discussion of this in Chapter 4). There is no national bourgeoisie in control of the state: there are ruling classes distributed across discontinuous institutions of global governance. Taking control of one or other of these may provide a tactical advantage for a short period, but without a systemic approach, neoliberal global governance will rapidly recuperate the loss.

Neoliberalism appears as a prison by enforcing the prism of national politics, and by encouraging the hopeless dream of national liberation. The national point of view is what makes neoliberalism seem powerful. And the recent functioning of the European Union allows us to see this clearly.

The European archipelago

At the outbreak of the Second World War, while still largely unknown and ignored, Friedrich Hayek wrote a paper that in recent years has seemed highly prescient in the contemporary European situation.[13] Writing well before the Treaty of Rome established the European Economic Community in 1957, in 'The Economic Conditions of Interstate Federalism' Hayek supports the idea of a federation of states on the basis that it would bring peace and that such a federation would frustrate all possibilities of state intervention in the economy and create an autonomous market, thereby leading to the disappearance of all political ideologies other than market subservience.[14] This is an integral element in bringing peace, according to Hayek's point of view, since he blamed these ideologies for causing war.

This neoliberal vision of 'peace' has come to replace many of the versions of peace that the European unification project originally stood for. What Hayek really seeks to do is transform potentially problematic, conflictual political citizens into pacified consumers – replacing political passion and concern for the common good with private interest, the choice between consumer goods, and a constant search for the cheapest price.

Hayek talks of an 'ideal' economic free trade area inside a federation. In such a free trade area, he says:

> The absence of tariff walls and the free movements of men and capital between the states of the federation ...

limit to a great extent the scope of the economic policy of the individual states. If goods, men, and money can move freely over the interstate frontiers, it becomes clearly impossible to affect the prices of the different products through action by the individual state.

It will also be clear that the states within the Union will not be able to pursue an independent monetary policy. With a common monetary unit, the latitude given to the national central banks will be restricted at least as much as it was under a rigid gold standard ...

Also, in the purely financial sphere, the methods of raising revenue would be somewhat restricted for the individual states. Not only would the greater mobility between the states make it necessary to avoid all sorts of taxation which would drive capital or labor elsewhere, but there would also be considerable difficulties with many kinds of indirect taxation.[15]

It is impossible today to read these lines as a European and not think of the restrictions on monetary policy created by the euro, which prevents countries such as Greece devaluing in order to deal with debts; to think of the way in which fiscal competition between EU states has driven down corporate taxation, and the way free movement of workers has been sometimes used to undermine wages and workers' rights; or to think of the European Semester and Fiscal Compact, whereby the European Commission controls the budgets of member states in a restrictive way, severely limiting the possibilities of state investment for Eurozone countries in deficit.

Even better from Hayek's point of view, he predicts this:

> Once frontiers cease to be closed and free movement is secured, all these national organisations, whether trade-unions, cartels, or professional associations, will lose their monopolistic position and thus, qua national organisations, their power to control the supply of their services or products.[16]

It is impossible today to read these lines as a European and not think of, for example, the way in which the infamous Viking and Laval judgments of the European Court of Justice concerning the posting of workers from one country to another undermine the possibility for strikes and other trade union action, or to think of the difficulty of coordinating a common position between unions of diverse member states.

There is an obvious objection to Hayek's predictions: surely the federal level will take on responsibilities for taxation and economic policy previously determined at the state level, thereby reintroducing democratic choice at a higher level? But Hayek says that this is unlikely, for one main reason that is the principal premise of his entire argument. Discussing tariffs, which he takes to be largely analogous to all forms of state intervention, he deploys this line of reasoning:

In the national state current ideologies make it compa-
ratively easy to persuade the rest of the community that
it is in their interest to protect 'their' iron industry or
'their' wheat production or whatever it be. An element
of national pride in 'their' industry and considerations
of national strength in case of war generally induce
people to consent to the sacrifice. The decisive conside-
ration is that their sacrifice benefits compatriots whose
position is familiar to them. Will the same motives
operate in favour of other members of the Union? Is
it likely that the French peasant will be willing to pay
more for his fertilizer to help the British chemical
industry? Will the Swedish workman be ready to pay
more for his oranges to assist the Californian grower?[17]

This reason, which he describes as the 'myth of nationality' that facilitates submission to the will of the majority,
is then reinforced by a further series of arguments based
on increased diversity in a federation: the more diverse
the federation is, the more difficult it is to impose any
economic constraints, because the diversity of people,
conditions and traditions means that it is less and less likely
that people will submit to any sacrifice. Ultimately, in such
a federation, Hayek rejoices that:

There seems to be little possible doubt that the scope for
the regulation of economic life will be much narrower
for the central government of a federation than for
national states. And since, as we have seen, the power

87

of the states which comprise the federation will be yet
more limited, much of the interference with economic
life to which we have become accustomed will be altogether impracticable under a federal organisation.[18]

Hayek's view is that it is only misguided ideologies,
linked with nationalism and war, that would lead otherwise rational individuals to 'help' each other by paying
more than the minimum price for goods that (he claims)
would exist if there were no state interference in economic
life. What prevents the emergence of a federal level of
governance is the persistence of these ideologies – albeit
disarmed and transformed by the market – which keep
individuals divided into nationalities, in competition both
individually with each other and collectively one country
against another. This is a stupendous logical reversal: precisely the nationalism that Hayek says enables solidarity and
intervention within a nation state is utilised to block its
emergence beyond it. Far from replacing national ideologies, neoliberalism is a parasite on them.

In this regard, Europe is little more than the most
obvious example of the transformation of the international
economic system over the last thirty years. Not too unlike
the workings of Hayek's ideal federation, international
capital exploits the fractures created by the breakdown of
the Bretton Woods system to play states off against each
other, enforcing a market logic on international relations
where the primary objective of each country, region, city
and town is to appear attractive in a global competition

for investment. Unless a country or city has a particularly strong starting position in this global race, and/or some particularly exceptional socio-political conditions, the winning combination tends to be an offer of lower wages, tax breaks and minimal contractual and environmental protections.[19]

It is precisely this logic of interstate competition that allows financial markets to act as the guard dogs of what is considered credible politics. 'Market confidence' – the disposition of highly mobile capital to camp in a given country – becomes an arbitrator of what is desirable, while electoral processes and the whims of social justice should not be allowed to interfere lest they scare investors away. It is not just the weaker countries that experience this. Nothing encapsulates Donald Trump's ambivalent relationship to 'globalisation' better than his agenda the day he relinquished the Trans-Pacific trade agreement. After killing the agreement in the morning, blaming it for the loss of US manufacturing jobs, he met the CEOs of some of the most important American corporations in the afternoon. During that meeting, the president reassured them that social, labour and environmental standards would be lowered in order to make it worthwhile reshoring production to the US. You can pick a free trade or nationalist approach, as long as you devalue labour. Or, as Henry Ford famously stated, you can have your Model T in any colour you want, as long as it is black.

Neoliberal 'globalism' and the national vision of politics go together – they are not opposites – and the former depends on the later. Hayek is ultimately proposing that the best way of limiting state intervention in the market would be to have an *economic federation combined with nationalised citizens*, unable to see beyond their national spheres, or to have any interest in collaborating with others outside their countries beyond the narrowest conception of trade.

Quoting William Morris, we may say that there is renewed truth in his dictum: 'modern nationalities are mere artificial devices for the commercial war that we seek to put an end to, and will disappear with it'.[20] Morris made these remarks in 1889, two years after the British government introduced compulsory 'country of origin' labelling to try to encourage British consumers to buy products 'made in Britain' rather than cheaper versions 'made in Germany'. Over time this strategy failed, as German goods in particular became associated with quality. Morris foresaw a time of neoliberalism when nations themselves would become commodities, and this is where Hayek's plans lead.[21]

To follow Hayek's argument we have to accept two things: firstly, that citizens 'help' each other *only* because of an ideological nationalism and not for any other reason; and secondly, that this form of nationalism would indeed not be superseded by any federal equivalent.

If Europe is the most advanced example of the functioning of this logic, it is also where this logic is being directly challenged – and the result of this challenge will have global implications. If you think that the European Union is unambiguously neoliberal, ask yourself these questions: is imposing a massive fine on Google neoliberal? Is legislating to impose maximum working hours? Or creating health and safety and food hygiene standards? Or using regional funds to invest in deprived areas? Some European legislation goes against the precepts of neoliberalism, and this is because the European Union is sufficiently strong to resist and propose alternatives. And, even more importantly, social and political processes carried forward by the citizens of Europe also show the falsity of Hayek's suppositions. The UK has been a leader in this, as we will now see.

We are the lions, Mr Manager[22]

> Hey sister, where are you going in the middle of the night?
> I'm going down to London, to the bloody Grunwick fight,
> Where a wee small band of immigrants are fighting
>   for their rights,
> So put your coat on, Jimmy man, and come and
> join the fight
> Hold the line! Hold the line!

So ran the song of the Grunwick movement in 1976. In August that year, Devshi Bhudia was fired from the Grunwick film-processing plant in north-west London for working too slowly packaging mail-order photographs. Three other workers walked out in support of him, and Jayaben Desai was dismissed for putting on her coat and preparing to join them. Her son walked out in protest and went to the local Citizens Advice Bureau, saying that they wanted to organise a picket and demand union representation. The events that unfolded over the coming two years represented one of the most important moments in the history of trade unions in the United Kingdom. What started as a small local dispute over unfair dismissals and unpaid compulsory overtime turned into a country-wide movement, with postmen refusing to process post from the Grunwick site, coalminers, steelworkers and thousands of other trade unionists coming from throughout the country to support the strike, and daily battles with the police. Prominent lawyers, doctors, journalists and politicians joined the picket, all supporting the right of workers in the film-processing plant to union representation.

What made the strike particularly important was that it was led by immigrant women, mostly from India, Pakistan, Bangladesh and East Africa, whom the media called 'Strikers in Saris'. The trade union with which they had been put in contact was the Association of Professional, Executive, Clerical and Computer Staff, a small, rather conservative union, unused to protesting, and certainly unaccustomed to representing Asian female workers. To their credit, by most accounts they did a good job of representing the strikers. The whole trade union movement in the United Kingdom engaged in a profound reflection on the rights of immigrant workers. The moment when white male workers stood in solidarity with the female, immigrant workers has been described as a watershed in race relations in the UK. The extent of the movement suggests that solidarity between workers is not national if nationalism implies a racist concept. Contrary to what Hayek might have anticipated, here were white British workers taking on costs for the benefit of immigrant workers, with the conviction that workers' rights benefit the whole workforce.

While the legacy of the movement has been transformational, in the short term the picket was unsuccessful, both in changing conditions in the factory and in changing the dominant attitudes of the trade union movement. The Labour government at the time refused to back the strikers, and the Trade Union Congress withdrew its support. Jayaben Desai was stripped of her trade union membership while on hunger strike outside the TUC in 1977. Two years later, Thatcher was elected and the 1980s saw a wholesale assault on trade union power. As coalminers and steelworkers who were involved in the Grunwick protests note to this day, it is striking that regular workers were able to see what was at stake at Grunwick, while the leadership of the unions and the Labour party could not – and all workers ultimately paid the price.

Fast-forward to the new millennium, and again immigrants are at the leading edge of the struggle for labour rights in the UK, and again it is women frequently leading that struggle. 'A living wage is important because we're people and we need to live a decent life.' For uttering these words in a campaign video, Susana Benavidez an Ecuadorian single mother working as a cleaner for Topshop in London, claims to have been fired. Her trade union,

United Voices of the World, is taking Britannia Service Group, which held the contract for cleaning services with Topshop, to an employment tribunal (Britannia disputes Susana's account). Susana is one of many migrant workers campaigning for an improvement in labour conditions in the United Kingdom, and often in the services industry. Justice for Cleaners campaigns have spread through London universities, initiated and often led by migrant workers, and supported by students coming from around the world.

The gig economy is another case in point, as the London Deliveroo and Uber strikes of 2016 and 2017 were largely led by migrants. What is more, protest in the gig economy is beginning to prefigure self-organised, transnational industrial action. After the initial wave of action in London had subsided, two unions got involved in organising with Deliveroo riders. The Independent Workers Union of Great Britain (IWGB), a small breakaway union formed in 2013, began to organise with workers in Camden in London, the epicentre of the summer strikes, and Industrial Workers of the World (IWW) engaged with workers nationally and in Bristol and Leeds in particular. Meanwhile, 'The Rebel Roo', a self-organised Deliveroo workers' bulletin, reached a membership of 1,500, or 10 per cent of the Deliveroo workforce. In October 2016, this model was replicated in Italy, with delivery workers in Turin staging coordinated protests against Foodora, the food delivery platform, in direct emulation of what was happening in the UK.[23] In Spain, Deliveroo workers went on strike in Barcelona, Valencia and Madrid on 2 July 2017. Participation was high, with nearly two-thirds of the Deliveroo workforce joining the strike. More recently, workers from the Netherlands, Austria and Greece have joined international organising meetings led by German, Italian and Spanish riders.[24] Back in the UK, in February 2017, the Transnational Social Strike Platform's assembly in London brought together 160 people from forty organisations and nine countries to discuss, organise and plan around questions on the social strike and coordinated transnational action in the gig economy,[25] with follow-ups in Berlin in July and in Turin in September.

Strikes and labour organisation are increasingly taking place across borders. Indeed, they have to in order to have an impact on today's leading employers and business models. Take Amazon, for example, which relies on a network of fulfilment centres, where goods are stored, packaged and shipped to customers. Amazon's alleged exploitation of workers to ensure its 'just in time' distribution chain is now well known, as is its market dominance. Since 2013, Verdi, a large German trade union, has been organising short-term strikes to try to pressure Amazon to respect Verdi's collective agreement on pay with Germany's mail order and retail industry. At times of high demand, however, Amazon has employed a simple mechanism to reduce the impact of these strikes: it uses its warehouses in Poland, across the border, to pick up the excess demand by requiring its workers to work overtime. In 2015, after several meetings between Amazon workers from Germany and Poland, the Amazon warehouses in Poznań struck back: when the management tried to require its workers in Poznań to work overtime during a strike organised by Verdi in Germany, the workers deliberately worked slowly. Several were dismissed as a result of this action, and the trade union representing them, Inicjatywa Pracownicza, is providing support for legal action against unfair dismissal as well as presenting demands to the management on higher pay. Inicjatywa Pracownicza (Workers' Initiative) is a new trade union and was chosen by the Amazon workers in Poznań impressed by its initiatives to support women workers in Poland, as well as by its logo of a fierce-looking cat. As in the case of gig economy workers, transnational coordination is just beginning but is growing, as the first simultaneous strike of Italian and German Amazon workers on Black Friday in November 2017 testifies.

Such cross-border action faces significant challenges, including hierarchies and partnerships between trade unions that stifle creative initiative (Verdi is traditionally partnered with Solidarność in Poland, for example, which would not support the workers' actions), employment practices that deliberately make it hard for workers to organise, a systematic weakening of labour law in most European countries, and the complexity of crossing linguistic and geographical barriers. On the other hand, the greater mobility of workers inside large corporations provides opportunities previous trade unionists may not have had. Many of those involved in industrial action in Poznań's

Amazon warehouse had been on training courses in the UK with workers from elsewhere in Europe, allowing the forming of links and a comparison of working conditions and pay: 'If we are the best workers in Europe, why are we the lowest paid?' several of the Polish workers pointedly asked their management on their return.[26] Indeed, the free movement of labour inside the European Union provides considerable opportunities for cross-border labour organisation and solidarity from below, just as much as legislation relating to posted workers and promoting competition from above makes traditional nationalised labour organising more difficult.[27] Actions such as those in Poznań show that solidarity exists between workers across Europe, and that solidarity is not merely a matter of charity, but a clear-headed political understanding that improving labour conditions in one place requires coordinated mobilisation with workers from elsewhere.

That awareness is now increasingly emerging in Europe. Indeed, once again we could tell the story of *two Europes*.

Striking a light

As soon as we announced the first activities of European Alternatives in London in 2007, people from across Europe and the world living in London wanted to organise with us, and people from throughout Europe living elsewhere contacted us about doing activities in their own cities. It was clear from the beginning that a civic, cultural and political organisation for a different European future was something that not only we had found missing from the landscape, but others were looking for as well. By 2010, it seemed important to gather as many of these people together as we could to talk about how to go forward, and so in September we organised a meeting in London for some 100 people from across the continent. The venue we chose for the meeting was Hanbury Hall, just around the corner from our makeshift offices in London's East End. It was cheap, nearby, and under threat of being transformed into luxury apartments, so it seemed a good choice. But it also had a significant history.

Hanbury Hall was originally built as a Huguenot chapel in 1719 by protestants fleeing Catholic France. Charles Dickens performed public readings in the hall in the nineteenth century, and, most importantly for us, it was the meeting place of the 'Match Girls' in 1888, who decided to protest against working conditions in the nearby Bryant and May matchstick factory by calling a 'strike'. The workers faced abusively long days, poor pay, fines for talking or going to the toilet, and health risks due to the phosphorous used in the factory. Many of the 1,200 women were Irish, many as young as twelve years old. They turned to the London Trades Council, formed to represent skilled tradesmen, and which had previously been reluctant to be associated with the poor, persuading (or shaming) it into supporting their action. They protested outside the Houses of Parliament, and with the help of leading socialist Annie Besant (later to become a member of the Indian National Congress, among other things), made a great deal of noise in the media. The success of these teenage girls and women, forcing concessions from their employer, led to the formation the Union of Women's Match Makers and was decisive in the formation of trade unions in Britain. Eleanor Marx, Herbert Burrows and other leading socialists and reformers addressed the Match Girls in Hanbury Hall, and so it seemed a highly appropriate place for our own modest initiative.

The Network gave European Alternatives the capacity to develop activities across the continent, for instance by evolving our London Festival of Europe into a Transeuropa Festival happening in many cities simultaneously. The Network has run campaigns on the rights of interns, new forms of trade unionism, precarity, and workers' rights in general in the European Union, and so the spirit of its founding location has remained with the Network. We saw that it is possible to mobilise citizens across the continent for common ends, and how this process requires the engagement of multiple actors and a great deal of bridge building.

One example comes from our work on the *commons*, where we took part in a movement demanding a new economic model beyond both state and the market. In 2009, the city of Paris had re-municipalised water as a common good. Soon after the Network was founded, a referendum in Italy saw the participation of over 27 million citizens demanding that water be considered a 'common good' and placed outside the reach of the market, and similar initiatives sprung up in Germany and elsewhere. Suddenly, the discourse on commons – already very present in European activist and academic circles – led to massive popular movements that stretched well beyond their original remit to include, for instance, culture. Several theatres were occupied in Italy under the slogan 'culture is a common good', among them the oldest theatre in Rome, Teatro Valle. One of the earliest activities of the Network was to spread this enthusiasm even further transnationally. We started from where it appeared most difficult – Eastern Europe – working with activists to develop a travelling caravan across the region – where 'commons' sounded too much like *communism* – which collaborated with local movements and initiatives to create a shared vocabulary able to bypass the constraints of the past. Indeed, we went even further afield: engaging in a one-year exchange that would bring European activists on the commons to China.[28] Back in Europe, activities in Serbia, Romania, Bulgaria and beyond and activists working on areas as diverse as the environment, digital rights, the cooperative economy and more were brought together to formulate a common set of ideas and demands. We worked to engage cities in the process, bringing together the mayors of Paris and Naples to show that municipalities could lead the way to a different type of economy. We even started drafting, together with several partners, a European Charter of the Commons, with the City of Naples passing legislation pledging to support it. The process continues to this day. In 2016, hundreds of activists met in the European Parliament in Brussels to set up the European Commons

Assembly, a transnational forum to coordinate a pan-European movement for the commons, and in October 2017 the Commons Assembly met for the second time as part of the Transeuropa Festival in Madrid. All in all, we saw that transnational solidarity was much more than talk, and much more than charity.

We don't want your charity

'We don't want your charity. We want you to understand you are in the same shit as us and for the same reasons! And then we want you to struggle with us!' These words were shouted by Christos, a Greek activist, at an organising meeting for Blockupy in the run-up to May 2015, when Blockupy coordinated protests in Frankfurt against the politics of the European Central Bank. These organising meetings were frequent, and, at the beginning of the process of bringing together the movement, a specific discourse of international solidarity was very much in evidence – a discourse that will be familiar to anyone from the global South who has attended international congresses. It came from activists in the north of Europe, who argued that, given that countries such as Germany and the Netherlands are the most economically powerful in Europe at the moment, activists from these countries have a specific obligation to help those from countries in the south of the continent suffering as a result of austerity politics. Very quickly, voices from the south (and others) protested against this vision of solidarity as a kind of 'help':

'We don't want your charity.' An analysis of the situation of mini-jobs[29] in Germany began, as well as an analysis of power, inequalities and economic wealth imbalances in the country, resulting in the discussion shifting from one of international charity to one of transnational solidarity. A realisation kicked in: that it is not so much that Germany has to help Greece or any of the other countries suffering from austerity, unemployment or poverty; rather, those on the losing end of these economic policies – be they citizens in Greece or the €400-a-month mini-jobber in Germany who doesn't count as an employee – need to join together in common advocacy for a different economic system to be implemented in the European Union. In this way, the process of building the Blockupy movement unmasked the neoliberal pretence that we are divided into nations, some of which may be more competitively successful than others and therefore have duties of charity to the 'losers'. Instead of this idea of competition, the appropriate way of conceiving of transnational solidarity is of struggle against a system that is unjust, and for which politics, not fate, is responsible, and which politics, not charity, must address.

Putting out the lights

Compare all this with the actions of 'official Europe', which gave a very different response to a similar Greek call for joint struggle. In the response to the European debt crisis, we see how neoliberal globalism, the anonymous functioning of the market, and nationalism work together to reinforce one another. This is visible in the response offered by the eighteen ministers sitting in the Eurogroup – the informal but all-powerful grouping of Eurozone finance ministers – to the Greek request for a new memorandum on debt following the victory of Syriza in 2015. 'Elections cannot be allowed to change economic policy,'[30] former German finance minister Wolfgang Schäuble famously said. 'We each have our own democracies, and the demands of one country cannot outweigh the demands of eighteen others.' His words illustrate the assumption that democracy only exists inside each country, that people are inevitably divided in national *demoi* with no common interest – and even though they might be *national* citizens, when it comes to having agency over common problems they are *citizens of nowhere*. This means that one national democracy cannot influence other national democracies, while simultaneously the route to a transnational democracy is barred. This frustrates any space for an alternative – nationally or transnationally. Indeed, the finance ministers involved did all they could to promote this vision of separate democracies in different countries: insulting and suspicious of each other, each with their own 'national interest' to defend. Instead of a genuine negotiation, of public reasoning in which opinions could be formed about the common good of Europeans, the European institutions were turned into secretive means of keeping people divided, telling populations that they were in a competition with untrustworthy competitors over scarce resources.

This mechanism serves to maintain the European Union as something close to Hayek's intuition: an intergovernmental semi-federation where interests are supposed to collide in secrecy through international negotiations conducted in rooms where the light never shines. Yet if the light did shine in such rooms, it would immediately be apparent that there is much common interest between the ruling elites, and that the spectacle of clashing interests is largely a show. This is the paradox that keeps neoliberalism alive: nationalism of the peoples combined with federated elites. It is no coincidence that governing elites are often so opposed to any proposal for greater democratisation of EU institutions and decision making, as the development of a transnational democracy would neutralise Hayek's trap of nationality and dismember their cherished mechanical Turk.

Indeed, the argument of a Conservative politician and philosopher such as Edmund Burke would appear revolutionary in today's Europe. In a 1774 address, delivered shortly after being elected MP for Bristol, he warned his electors thus:

Parliament is not a congress of ambassadors from different and hostile interests; which interests each must maintain, as an agent and advocate, against other agenda and advocates; but parliament is a deliberative assembly of one nation, with one interest, that of the whole; where, not local purposes, not local prejudices, ought to guide, but the general good, resulting from the general reason of the whole. You choose a member indeed; but when you have chosen him, he is not member of Bristol, but he is a member of parliament.[31]

The development of such common interest is precisely what interstate diplomacy attempts to frustrate – often, as we will see, directly frustrating the demands of Europe's only directly elected parliament.

'We are not forming coalitions of states, we are uniting men,' said Jean Monnet, one of Europe's early architects.[32] By applying the unhappy strategy of neoliberalism in recent years – economic federation combined with blinkered nationalism – the European Union has come to resemble a prison system in which each people is in solitary confinement and each prisoner another prisoner's guard. The result is an archipelago penitentiary system promising misery for the many and impunity for the thieves.

The pirate federation

The warm hug offered by the driver left Tove stunned. Taxi rides often provide a barometer for political sentiment in a city, but this time there was little chit-chat during the ride to Brussels airport, and little concession to apparently more popular debates on the corruption of the political class or the never-ending negotiations between the French and Flemish minorities. Tove, a seasoned international campaigner with the European Network on Debt and Development, had been speaking about tax havens.

The topic of multinational tax dodging is fast becoming mainstream. Tove's previous work was in climate justice: she switched over because she was 'tired of being told there is no money'. And the scandalous scale of tax dodging pierces through this false narrative. Numbers don't usually make for an appealing communication strategy, but one very small number recently did: 0.005 per cent. This was the tax rate for much of Apple's European profits thanks to a sweetheart deal with the Irish state. It is not unique. A fierce competition to the bottom is pushing European governments to lower taxation for large businesses in order to attract them to their jurisdiction and 'steal' taxes from their neighbours, all the while creating unfair competition for small- and medium-sized enterprises (SMEs).[33] And the competition is, of course, global, with the US and European states entering a race in 2017 on lowering the official tax rate.

Tax havens may sound like a tropical affair, but you are just as likely to find oak trees and beer as palm trees and rum: Europe has at least four such tax heavens – eight if you count British dependencies.[34] We know well how the system works, just as we know what should be done to stop it. The procedures vary from country to country, but the two most common ones have evocative names: *double Irish* and *Dutch sandwich*. The names are important, as they remind us that national governments are in charge of the scam. The double Irish (soon to be replaced by the new 'patent box', similar in all but name) is used by companies as varied as Apple, Google, Pfizer, Adobe, Johnson &

Johnson and Yahoo!, and requires registering two separate companies in Ireland: one to collect European profits and one to hold the patents for the products sold. The first company will then pass most of the profits to the second in the form of royalties – that is, rights to use the patent. Thanks to special legislation reserved for royalty payments received by Irish-based multinational corporations, the second company will avoid nearly all taxes. And so the cash piles up in the Republic of Ireland. What, then, happens to all this money? Wiring it back to, say, the United States would mean paying US corporate tax, which, although low, is still a significant percentage. A better idea is to transfer it where the number is a perfect zero: Bermuda. However, a direct bank transfer would be taxed, as there is a slight levy on exporting profits from the Irish Republic. Cleverly, this law applies only to non-EU transfers and – guess what? – in some EU countries, such as the Netherlands, this law does not exist. Thus a small detour is necessary, a stopover in the profitable flight to tax immunity (first-class tickets only). Let's take the example of Google. Like Apple, it has a double structure in Ireland. The patent company transfers profits to Google Netherlands Holdings BV, the Dutch branch office (number of employees: zero). This branch, in turn, reverses 99.8 per cent of what it receives to Google Ireland Holdings, which has its registered office ... in Bermuda. Ireland–Netherlands–Bermuda: here is the new triangle responsible for the disappearance of much of the corporate tax otherwise payable by some of the most profitable companies on the planet.

Many European multinationals are involved in the same game. Among them is the Swedish giant Ikea, accused of dodging over €1 billion of taxes by shifting European profits to its Dutch branch and from there to Luxembourg, where out of €15.6 billion it paid a paltry €477 million, or 3 per cent, in tax.[35] A rather inexpensive bill compared with what SMEs are asked to pay.

The European Parliament and European Commission are well aware of the injustices this system produces. The parliament, notably, in its attempt to represent the interests of the 'whole', has long been pushing for greater tax harmonisation and stricter regulations against tax evasion. As Tove says, 'a harmonised tax base should not be utopian and it's not rocket science'. However, so far nothing has been agreed except superficial reform. Why? A report[36] from the European Parliament explains it well, noting that there is a widespread pattern of systematic obstruction among national states to limit any action against tax evasion and to conceal information, with states regularly jealously protecting their corporate sweethearts and their cosy deals,[37] all the while searching for new 'niche markets' they can occupy. It is a tough race: while Ireland specialises in high-tech and the Netherlands in financials, small Portugal has decided to leverage an asset its northern competitors do not have – the sun. And so it has started promoting tax-free status to European elders wishing to move their residency – and their untaxed pension – to Europe's West Coast.

While states work to outcompete one another in a self-defeating race to the bottom, citizens are increasingly in the fast lane. Tove is just one representative of a widespread transnational movement for tax justice that sees through the trap of nationality.

Again, it is the very logic of interstate diplomacy that makes multinational tax evasion such a hard beast to fight. As Tove argues, 'Who do you bring demands to?' Given that all decisions follow a strictly intergovernmental procedure, she has neither a clear enemy nor a clear interlocutor. 'Should I hope the European Council has one of their secret meetings and solves the problem?' she asks rhetorically. The European Union's intergovernmental system serves precisely to transform power into a ghost, seemingly absent and yet incredibly effective in reducing the political agency of organised citizenry. The invisible hand of the market has become the invisible hand of a captured political class, one that uses the prism of the nation to divide and rule over their citizens. We see there is nothing inevitable about it, nothing natural – rather, it is a political ploy that more and more citizens are beginning to unmask. And it is the result of this struggle that will define the world to come.

Europe as metaphor for the world to come

'How did you feel as I was reading the poem?' asks Pablo Neruda. 'It's weird … the words went back and forth, like the sea … I felt seasick … I felt like a boat tossing around on those words,' replies Ruoppolo. At the end of this famous dialogue from the film *Il Postino*, Neruda asks his new friend with a smile, 'Do you know what you have done, Mario? ... You've invented a metaphor!'

We have insisted from the beginning of this book that Europe has always been a metaphor, a myth through which we can understand our predicament in its promise and in its violence. But there is a space of agency inside the myth that is really about us, readers and citizens.

If the most politically and economically integrated continent reverts to a situation of opposing nation states pitted against each other, this will be a dramatic preview of the new global disorder to come. It will, in effect, be the surrendering of a continent to the worldview of neoliberalism, in which civic agency and human autonomy are replaced by the fake automaticity of markets and the consumption and commodification of everything. If, on the other hand, Europe turns into a giant nation state, with even greater state powers for control within and projection of power abroad, saying 'Europe first' and militarising its borders, then Europe's horizon of politics is simply more of the same on a larger scale.

If, however, Europe were able to build a real politics beyond borders, if it were able to demonstrate that unity of action across national divisions were possible, and that a politics centred on citizens who cross borders is possible, this could transform the world. We do not mean, simply, that a politically united Europe would be 'large enough' to have its voice heard in the international arena. That, in itself, may mean very little, or even be counterproductive. Donald Trump, after all, also has a big voice. But here is the rub: firstly, for Europe to *acquire* such a voice – for Europe to become a credible political actor – it needs to surpass the inconclusive cacophony of intergovernmental diplomacy, the competition between states. This is the very system that at once traps it in an economic status quo and paralyses any serious joint initiative, resulting in unjust as much as ineffective politics. And secondly, for this European voice to be genuinely different, it would be the voice *of citizens* in their diversity, and not of *the state*, of the administration and its bordered thinking. We will say much more about this in Chapter 4 of this book, where we introduce a new form of transnational political party as the vehicle through which transnational democracy can emerge in an interdependent world, but for the moment the point is that the establishment of a transnational democracy in Europe, in and of itself, would undo one of the most powerful mechanisms through which the subservience of politics to the markets operates. In the examples we have seen above, it is the citizens in the fast lane who need to win. Given the size and economic significance of the European Union, this would be a move with global implications. Let us list some of them.

From competition to cooperation

It would mean, for instance, accomplishing Tove's objective of developing a common taxation policy that would remove tax havens from the European continent. A move such as this would immediately reverberate throughout the rest of the world. Once Europe overcomes its addiction to – and fake national interest in – tax dodging, it is then a small step to shut out the remaining pirate island states and lead a global reorganisation of tax regimes. The point can be generalised: at national level we lack serious mechanisms for fairly taxing wealth concentration. This results in European states fighting over the crumbs, aspiring at best to increase public deficits. If the international system tolerates and indeed makes possible organised robbery, we cannot be content with fighting for what's left over in the till.

Similarly, a genuine European financial transaction tax could apply to any bank trading in Europe or transacting with a European bank, thereby having a massive global impact in bringing traceability and accountability to a system constantly at risk of spiralling out of control, as well as generating public revenue.

What is interesting about both proposals is that they would work most effectively if they were directly managed by European authorities. Imagine a common European tax for, say, internet giants and for financial transactions. This would create a significant pool of resources that previously simply disappeared offshore; and, at the same time, it would provide the EU with an independent budget for investment and social programmes, creating the financial space for the 'common interest' of Europeans.

Undoing the 'divide and rule' that keeps Eurozone nations laced into the straitjacket of a common monetary union accountable to no one would signify politicising European economic policy, replacing the automaticity of fiscal parameters and outdated rules on deficit and debt with a public, cross-national conversation on how one of the world's largest treasuries should operate. Creating a common budget for the Eurozone under the democratic oversight of its citizens would mean opening up the possibility of common investment on a scale sufficient to upgrade our production model and have an impact on the world's economy: think ecological reconversion.

A transnational Europe would mean recognising that some kinds of goods are essential to human life and should be kept out of the market and governed in a highly participatory way: water, culture, forests and energy, among others, are common goods that are not always best managed by the state, which are exploited by the market, and by their nature often cross borders. By removing common goods from the market, Europe would be undoing some of the fundamental ways in which the nexus between neoliberalism and the state dispossesses citizens of essential goods, as well as creating democratic governance structures for these goods that should also be open to others from outside the European Union. The European Commons Assembly is prefiguring these changes.

Neither Silicon Valley nor the Great Firewall of China

Or let us think about technology. In the span of ten years, the top five US companies by market capitalisation have all changed – except one (Microsoft). Out go the car makers and big electricity providers; in come Google, Amazon, Apple and Facebook. American dominance over the digital economy is all but uncontested. With a single exception: again, China. This is the only other digital ecosystem where corporate giants compete for world leadership and influence the future of our digital standards. Chinese giants such as Tencent and Alibaba challenge the market capitalisation of Google and Amazon, and for every Facebook there is a Renren, for every Twitter a Weibo, for every eBay a JD.com. This is a digital race from which Europe is peculiarly absent.[38] As authors, we are not particularly worried about this in itself – we are not, after all, European nationalists, and this is not a book about making Europe great again. However, a democratic Europe would empower its citizens to refuse the false choice between Silicon Valley and the Great Firewall of China, the blackmail between having our data harvested and monetised by big US corporations and the National Security Agency, or by big Chinese corporations and the Communist Party. We do not need a 'nationalist' internet of our own. The challenge is rather to build the internet the world needs. We would be able to *take back control* over the choice of how our digital ecosystems operate, drastically reconceptualising our approach to data – the new oil of the twenty-first century – and decide whether natural digital monopolies should be treated like public utilities. Whether, for instance, data has to be treated as a commons and taken back into public control, so corporations can have access to it for a fee but can never own it.[39] We need to be empowered not only to *decide* collectively on these matters through democratic institutions, but to enact and create these alternative forms of digital commons through our actions and interactions, through the possibility of creating new kinds of cooperative forms for our businesses, and legal forms for property held in common.

Pulling people up, not down

Europe's market remains the largest in the world, which potentially gives it enormous leverage. This means that accomplishing the vision of Jayaben or Christos or the transnational strikers in the gig economy would mean creating genuine transnational labour policies as well as transnational unions that would guarantee the reversal of social dumping, pulling up wages and standards towards the top rather than racing to the bottom. It would mean that the EU's trade agreements could work to civilise neoliberal globalisation by ensuring decent pay and working conditions both inside and outside the EU, rather than simply prioritising the opening of free markets, as is currently the case. This would be a much-needed example for other parts of the world. Think of the race to the bottom between the USA and Mexico, where Mexican wages are depressed in order to incite delocalisation of production, with a lose–lose result for workers on both sides of the border.

A transnational Europe would mean democratising international trade law, the development of which is currently driven by corporations and big business. Instead of secretive trade negotiations or arbitration panels deciding on disputes between corporations and states, a democratic Europe would have the resources to promote open and transparent processes and agreements that citizens and NGOs can access. International trade law benefits corporations for as long as states are divided and can be played off against each other, since the jurisprudence tends to favour the activist corporation – the international settlements and dispute system, the international courts arbitrating between corporations and states now built into thousands of trade deals, is a case in point. Transnational civil society organisations working for the common good must be able to drive the judicial process of international trade law codification, not shut out of the courtrooms. Jurisprudence is too important to be left to corporations, governments and judges. Europe could make this change in the paradigm of international trade deals: activist citizens, not activist corporations, must be empowered in the new transnational politics.[40] Democracy must catch up with trade: where companies are trading and investing across borders, parliaments need to be working together across borders to ensure that laws governing trade protect the public interest. The European Parliament could be the first transnational parliament to do this, welcoming delegations from other parliaments to jointly decide on these matters.

Metaphors have real-world effects, even in that most unpoetic of realms, the global economy. If we can understand Europe going beyond the fake opposition between nationalism and neoliberal globalism, if we see it as the signifier that our lives are neither local nor global, but rather intertwined in multiple webs of solidarity, similarities of circumstances and common interests that require collaboration and creativity, then Europe opens up spaces of transnational struggle that make economic transformation possible. In the last chapter we will see how this space can be opened wide, how we can make the vision of a transnational democracy appear a realistic prospect and not a daydream.

Citizens going beyond the nation state in Europe would transform the world in a more profound sense as well: they would transform the kind of political actors that exist in the world, and change the relationship between self, other and world. The unity of Europe cannot be the kind of unity that is found in the nation, only writ larger and with more power. The unity of Europeans must be based on genuinely going across borders, a radical development of the meaning of citizenship itself. This, then, is where we now turn.

Chapter 3

If Europe Is a Fortress
We Are All in Prison

We live in a world in which human beings as such
have ceased to exist for quite a while; since society has
discovered discrimination as the great social weapon
by which one may kill men without any bloodshed;
since passports or birth certificates, and sometimes
even income tax receipts, are no longer formal papers
but matters of social distinction.

Hannah Arendt, 'We refugees', 1943[1]

Face to face with the unbearable inequality
of free movement

If you take a train from northern Italy to the south of
France – from Milan to Nice, for example – you will stop
at Ventimiglia, the last station in Italy before the train
continues into Monaco and then France. As you sit in your
carriage, it is possible – likely, even, at some times of the

year and at night – that a man will approach you and ask if he can hide among your luggage. You suspect he might not have the legal right to be in the European Union and to move around freely. What should you do? Tell him to get lost? Try to ignore him but allow him to hide in your luggage if he wants to? Call the police? Help him to hide?

It is likely that each of us knows what we would do in such a situation. But whichever option you choose, the rest of your journey is likely to be troubled. Instead of looking through the window at the Mediterranean and daydreaming, you are likely to be reflecting on the plight of those who attempt perilous journeys across it. You may worry about the fate of the man whose path you crossed. Or you may be worried that the man hiding in your luggage will be discovered and that you might get in trouble as a result ...

The European migration crisis poses an existential question to those of us who are among the fortunate ones: what justifies *our* being in the European Union and having freedom of movement when that right is denied to so many who have the most need of movement (those fleeing war, persecution or poverty, for example)? When migration was not such a visible drama, this question was not posed by many, but scenes of people drowning in the Mediterranean, being held in often unacceptable conditions at detention centres or camps, trying to scale barbed-wire fences in Melilla or Ceuta, avoiding the army at the Hungarian, Macedonian or Bulgarian borders, or gassed by French police in Calais makes this question inescapable for all but the most wilfully blind. Faced with this question, some people try to justify that rights apply to some and not to others on the basis of natural merit (i.e. those born here to the right parents) or natural deficiency (i.e. those born elsewhere); they may project their fears onto strangers and see in them a danger, always finding enough evidence to supposedly justify their fears. Others may find scenarios such as the one we imagined in the train as all too reminiscent of some of the worst moments in Europe's history, and worry that Europe is rolling back up the same track.

The lack of a humane European migration policy means that there is no perfect answer to what you ought to do in the train. Without any confidence that the legal system will grant asylum even to those who should have that right under the Geneva Convention, it is difficult to justify handing the man over to the authorities. At the same time, you do not even know if the man is a refugee, let alone the reason he is trying to cross the border. In real-life scenarios such as the momentary decision that needs to be made on that train, there is no time or means for finding out answers. Probably the only justifiable thing to do is help him hide in one way or another, but this is only a calculation based on probability and not on certitude, and it may turn out to be the wrong decision. Even if it is morally the right decision, you might end up in trouble should a police officer decide that you are aiding irregular migration. This tension mixed with shame is the intolerable position that we privileged Europeans are forced into, with each of us effectively turned into border control officers. This at a time when even the real border control officers are often uncertain about what they are supposed to be doing, torn between their human responsibilities for others, often incoherent and contradictory instructions from above, and occasional calls for hostility. Of course, the situation is much worse for the migrants themselves – what is mere uncertainty for privileged Europeans is too often a matter of life and death for those making dangerous journeys. It is important, though, to see that this common European uncertainty and even shame is perhaps at the root of widely divergent public attitudes towards migration. Thus, addressing the failure of politics that is behind this uncertainty is crucial in addressing the 'migration crisis'. This has never been a crisis of numbers – the number of migrants arriving in Europe is very small in comparison with the European population; it has always been a crisis in European attitudes, which in turn becomes a life or death crisis for many migrants.

Schizophrenia

The thought experiment we just conducted is a daily reality for many people living in the border regions of Europe. The cases of Pierre-Alain Mannoni and Cédric Herrou at the French–Italian border and the legal trials that have followed them in 2017 are examples that reveal a public and legal schizophrenia when it comes to migration.

On 17 October 2016, Pierre-Alain Mannoni, a university researcher in Nice, went for dinner with friends in the Roya Valley, between Italy and France. He had heard about an unused building belonging to the French railway company SNCF being used to house migrants in the valley. Previously it had been a holiday complex for railway workers, but it had been unused since 1991 until activists occupied it to provide shelter a few days before Mannoni stopped by on his drive back to Nice. At 1am in the morning, he saw a building with no water or electricity, housing around sixty people. Among them were three young female Eritreans who had injuries on their legs, and he was asked if he could drive them to Marseille so that they could get medical attention. As they were cold, young, vulnerable and injured, he agreed. His car was stopped and confiscated at La Turbie on the French border, where he was put in handcuffs and detained for 'helping the circulation, entry, and stay of foreigners in an irregular situation', an accusation that can lead to five years' imprisonment and a €30,000 fine. On 23 November, the public prosecutor in Nice called for Mannoni to be punished as 'a severe warning: offering aid is an obligation, but facilitating the circulation across borders is a crime. These actions do not correspond to offering aid, but rather to denying that borders between countries exist and that a country can decide on its laws.' The tribunal of Nice did not follow the advice of the public prosecutor; rather, it judged that Mannoni was acting to preserve the dignity of the young Eritreans. Reacting to this decision, the mayor of Nice, Christian Estrosi, claimed that it 'puts French people at risk'. The public prosecutor took the case to the court of appeal, where, in September 2017, Mannoni was sentenced to a two-month suspended prison sentence. Mannoni has announced that he will appeal this decision.

The centre for migrants in the disused SNCF holiday home that Mannoni had visited was opened by Cédric Herrou, among others. Herrou is a farmer in the Roya Valley who regularly accompanies migrants across the border and gives them shelter. In February 2017, the court in Nice imposed a €3,000 fine for transporting migrants from Ventimiglia into France. The public prosecutor appealed, and in August he was condemned by the Aix appeal court to a four-month suspended prison sentence. The Nice court had pardoned Herrou of illegally occupying the SNCF building, but the appeal court ordered him to pay €1,000 to the railway company in damages. The court said Herrou had provided no evidence that the people he was helping were in danger. Reacting to the judgment, Herrou said:

> I'd invite the members of the court to come to the Roya Valley and speak to the families of the fifteen people who have died trying to cross the border. I will continue to fight. If they want to stop me, they should put me in prison, it would be simpler … where the state fails, the citizens have an obligation to act.

Both Herrou's and Mannoni's cases were closely followed by the French public, and the contradictory judgments of the different courts reflect an ambiguity in a crucial law: specifically, the law recognises that humanitarian aid to preserve the dignity of people, offer them medical assistance or keep them out of harm is legal, but it criminalises assisting in the crossing of borders.

This ambiguity has a long history in France, intertwined with the history of human rights. At the beginning of the French Revolution, the country offered citizenship to all those wanting to escape tyranny and live in freedom. But by 1793, France was at war and, afraid of enemy infiltrators, the National Convention made it illegal to hide from the authorities someone subject to migration laws. Fast-forward to the beginning of the twentieth century, and France was the European country that welcomed the most migrants – and it received even more after the First World War. In the 1930s, in the context of economic hardship and the Great Depression, voices started to be raised against refugees fleeing Nazi Germany, Fascist Italy and elsewhere. In 1938, the government made it punishable by law to facilitate the entry and stay of irregular migrants. This law was the direct inspiration for the law of 1941 in occupied Paris, which required that 'anyone hosting a Jew should declare this within twenty-four hours to the police'. In 1945, in liberated France, the law of 1938 was again proclaimed, word for word, and since then several laws have made the punishments more and more severe.

In 2012, under the presidency of François Hollande, the government promised to abolish 'the crime of solidarity' ('*délit de solidarité*') in the country of Liberty, Equality and Fraternity. Thus, the law was amended so that if the act is not in return for payment, and if it consists of legal advice, medical aid or any other assistance to preserve the dignity of the person, then it cannot be punished by law. Yet the law maintains the article which says that helping someone cross the border is illegal and can be punished by a €30,000 fine. Thus, legal schizophrenia is created in a situation where helping someone cross the border is an essential part of preserving their dignity as a person.

Under political and public pressure, the courts judging Herrou and Mannoni have vacillated between solidarity and punishment, between hospitality and borders. It is through this vacillation that Herrou and Mannoni are subject to legal harassment, never totally capable of clearing their names.

This Kafkaesque pattern is repeated in other European countries. Under the guise of fighting people trafficking, the Italian authorities have tried to outlaw the work of NGOs saving lives in the Mediterranean. Elsewhere, putting up militarised walls in the Balkans is presented as saving the lives of migrants, who then drown in dangerous sea crossings elsewhere. Holding migrants in Libya, where they are subject to violence, rape and torture, is held up as sparing them a dangerous journey ... This is a policy area of such confusion that everything starts to mean its opposite, and the only people who profit from this topsy-turvy situation are those who want to exploit the migrants by either trafficking them, supplying the weaponry to states to militarise their borders, or turning their suffering into political gain through a game of 'Who can sound the most brutal?'

Let us look more closely at the overall European response and how confused and dangerous it has been allowed to become.

The official European response: a denial of reality

The European governmental response to the recent increase in irregular migration has been inexcusable, and when looked at from the point of view of other countries, highly cynical. The United Nations estimates that, by the end of 2015, 65 million people were displaced globally, and over 85 per cent of these people are living in poorer countries such as Tunisia, Turkey, Jordan, Lebanon and Palestine. Over 1 million migrants arrived 'irregularly' in Europe in 2015, but Europe has a population of over 500 million and is one of the richest places on earth. Since 2015, the number of arrivals in Europe has been reduced – held up as a success by politicians trying to avoid the problem, but in reality simply indicating that more of those fleeing for protection are having to look elsewhere. This is a shameful situation for the European Union, which claims to be founded on the value of respect for human dignity and human rights (Article 2 of the Treaty on European Union).

For a brief, glorious moment in the summer of 2015, Angela Merkel tried to act as a real leader of Europe, declaring the situation a humanitarian emergency, explaining to Germany's citizens the moral imperative of offering welcome, acknowledging that this would be challenging, but assuring that 'we can do it'. Unfortunately, the German state was unready to welcome significant numbers of migrants and faced problems upscaling its capacity quickly. Above all, in an extraordinary reversal of roles, it was Germany's turn to experience what Greece had already involuntarily tested; an intergovernmental system that incentivises short-termism and national egotism meant that a number of other countries turned against Merkel's moral lead, shut their borders and declared the idea of 'opening the doors of Europe' irresponsible and reckless.

More and more migrants became stranded on Greek islands, and, faced with some European member states simply blocking any solution that called on them to accept refugees, Merkel found herself pushed into championing an immoral, inhumane, ineffective and politically reckless EU agreement with Turkey in March 2016. This deal treats humans as if they were commodities to be traded – a 'bad' refugee who arrived irregularly on the Greek islands traded against a 'good' refugee who arrived in Turkey – and while it may have reduced crossings in the Aegean, it has done little to resolve the problems in Greece, has left many asylum seekers in dangerous hands in Turkey while emboldening its demagogic president Erdoğan, and has contributed to increasingly dangerous journeys along other routes. Above all, it has done little to ensure that those people who need asylum can get it, with the objectives of the political class in Europe being simply to try to stop people arriving rather than to welcome people fleeing to safety. Even so, the Turkey deal is being held up as a successful way of dealing with the problem, to be copied with even more dangerous countries for migrants such as Libya.

It did not have to be this way. The migration flows and deaths in the Mediterranean and on other European borders did not start suddenly in 2015, and it was predictable that at some point there would be increased migration waves coming from war-torn, politically unsettled neighbouring countries, and countries experiencing environmental and poverty problems. At least since the arrival of up to 20,000 Albanians on the *Vlora* cargo ship in the port of Bari, Italy, in 1991, it has been clear that emergency migration flows to Europe were entering a new era. During the Yugoslav wars, without a Common European Asylum System, without Frontex, without a European Refugee Fund, Europe was able to organise asylum for Bosnians, Kosovars, Croats, Serbs and others, even if the European response in stopping genocide was left wanting. The various ad hoc mechanisms for managing and welcoming emergency flows of refugees created during these years were packaged by the European Commission in the Temporary Protection Directive of 2001, which sought to establish a quick way of providing protection to people unable to return to their countries, particularly where the influx was submerging the asylum system. Scandalously, at no point during or since 2015 has there been any serious discussion of using this already-existing legislation. If it had been proposed by the European Commission forcefully and early, and those receiving protection were issued with Schengen visas, it would have genuinely Europeanised the issue. Instead of this paradigm shift, the Commission's solution was to renationalise the problem through quotas for each member state, which makes each national government central again, capable of blocking the system by non-application. Instead of acknowledging the agency of the migrants themselves, who would move to where they could be most adequately welcomed and find work, the inter-national response confines them to the state where they arrived, creating unmanageable concentrations in entry countries. It is as if the European governments do not want to find a solution, and wish the problem would simply go away.

While the political classes have been burying their heads in the sand, civil society groups have been highly mobilised in promoting solidarity with those fleeing war, poverty or climate change. The heartening sight of thousands of volunteers going to help refugees arriving on Europe's shores and at train stations, the refugee welcome campaigns and the many thousands of welcome initiatives and projects are fruits of a long tradition of civil society showing hospitality. Once again, we see *two Europes* existing side by side.

The best hotel in Europe

Take a look at the website for the City Plaza hotel in Athens and you will see the following slogan: 'No pool, no minibar, no room service but still the best hotel in Europe!'[2]

The City Plaza hotel had been empty for years when it was reopened on 22 April 2016 by activists from across Europe as a free hotel welcoming migrants. Upon arrival, migrants and asylum seekers are registered according to whether they are seeking asylum in Greece, whether they want to join the European relocation programme, or whether they are waiting to be reunited with their family somewhere else in Europe. There are up to 400 migrants at any one time, usually around half of whom are children. And dozens of volunteers who have come from across the continent to help and who now occupy the sixth floor of the building.[3]

Experiences such as the City Plaza abound in Europe. Rome, the Italian capital, strikingly lacks any official structure to welcome and provide orientation to migrants arriving through the dangerous Mediterranean route. The gap has been filled, once again, by citizens acting where the institutions fail. The Baobab centre aids hundreds of migrants every day without any public support – just the relentless work of volunteers who hand out clothing and food, organise temporary accommodation, and offer legal and psychological aid. We could tell endless stories like these.

Beyond providing a necessary welcome and showing Europe's humane face, civil society started proposing solutions well before the European leaders paid any attention to the issues surrounding irregular migration. To take but one example, following the migrant shipwreck of 3 October 2013 which saw over 360 people die, hundreds of European civil society groups and social movements agreed to meet on the island of Lampedusa to do precisely that which European states were blatantly refusing to do: offer a political response. The result was the Charter of Lampedusa, which the authors of this book participated in drafting: a comprehensive document that starts by recognising that our political institutions need to be remade to take into account the reality of human mobility, and that articulates the paradigm shifts in citizenship, education, healthcare, labour, family law and other areas of political life which this implies.[4]

In contrast to the far-sightedness of European civil society, the official European response to the migration crisis is premised on a denial of reality. It is based on the idea that, firstly, migration flows are only temporary and, secondly, it is possible to make the route into Europe so dangerous that people will prefer to go elsewhere or stay put. We know that these premises are totally unrealistic as well as being immoral. Migration to Europe is not going to stop any time soon – war, environmental changes and economic reasons will mean that migration to Europe will only increase, while at the same time the distinction between 'economic migration' and migration based on persecution, violence or war is going to become less and less clear-cut. Short of putting gunboats in the Mediterranean and fully militarising the borders, it is difficult to see how the route can be made so dangerous that many people will not attempt it, given that they are already taking huge risks. The European strategy supposedly dealing with the issue can be summed up as 'out of sight, out of mind'. Governments attempt to block passage so that asylum seekers cannot arrive on European soil and so they do not become a 'European responsibility'; asylum seekers and other migrants are detained in detention camps out of public view; and governments attempt to put up walls and barriers, as if that would make the issue go away.

Citizens organising beyond borders are instrumental in ensuring that the plight of migrants is neither out of sight nor out of mind. Our experience with migrant detention centres offers an example of that.

Open access

Estimates of the number of asylum seekers and irregular migrants being held in detention centres across Europe vary from around 50,000 to several hundred thousand.[5] At least 390 migrant detention centres in Europe and at its borders are known to exist.[6] This information is difficult to unearth, because governments do not release it, and so researchers and activists try to piece together an overview through visits and interviews. In general, very little is known about the places in which people can be detained for nothing more than being accused of breaking the border laws. This is quite deliberate: governments would prefer that their citizens do not know too much, and do not think too much either, about the conditions in which they detain men, women and often children for months – up to eighteen months in most European countries, and indefinitely in some countries, such as the UK, that have opted out of EU-agreed limits. This does not just concern non-European migrants: in the UK, over 4,500 European citizens suspected of committing immigration-related offences are estimated to have been detained in 2016, with the number increasing dramatically since 2009.[7] While governments would prefer that journalists, NGOs and the general public do not know too much about these centres, at the same time they are counting on people released from detention to spread the word. While detention centres are a very ineffective way of removing people from the country – in the UK and Italy, for example, it was estimated that over half of the people detained are eventually released without removal – they may contribute to creating a 'hostile environment' for migration, and a deterrent.[8]

In 2010, European Alternatives ran one of its first major activities in Paris along with the network Migreurop – a summit of migration activists from across the continent to discuss the 'Stockholm programme' of the European Union, which set the European framework for EU action on migration and asylum between 2009 and 2014. Coming soon after the adoption of the 'return directive' in 2008, which made it easier for member states to expel and detain non-EU migrants, it was clear that the direction of European policy was towards a toughening of the border regime. After hearing from doctors about the dangerous conditions in several migrant detention centres, we decided that over the coming years we should run a public awareness campaign on this issue.

But how to go about it? Migreurop had managed to map the existence of many detention centres, but getting inside and finding out information are not easy. In some member states no one is allowed in, while in other countries only certain NGOs have permission, and they have an interest in keeping their exclusive access granted by the government (and so may be reluctant to release particularly damning information). We knew that members of both the European and national parliaments automatically have the right to enter detention centres – and so the campaign idea was born: we would mobilise journalists and civil society organisations to request access to detention centres across Europe and in its borderlands. If access was refused, then we would mobilise members of parliament to go to the centres and look inside, attempting to take journalists and civil society representatives with them. Those people who were able to go inside the centres would document what they saw, which areas they were allowed to access, and which areas they were not.

Over 2011 and 2012, in several waves, we conducted the campaign 'Open Access Now', making requests to enter detention centres in towns and in the countryside, in airports (at customs control) and in ports, on the European mainland, and in Turkey, Melilla, Ceuta, Morocco and Mauritania. In some countries, journalists were able to go in. In most they were not; and in some, including France and Bulgaria, journalists who tried to take photographs outside the camp faced intimidation and even arrest. The motives given by the authorities for refusing access, where they were given at all, were often highly questionable: the emergency situation created by the influx of migrants following the Arab Spring, for example, or upcoming elections in a country. The 'risk of revolt' caused by visits of people external to the camp was frequently used as a reason to refuse access in Italy, while in Romania the 'violence of the detainees' was cited. In Belgium, the authorities denied access to the centres journalists had asked about but suggested they visit a new centre, which was still totally empty.

The conditions seen by those people who were allowed inside were frequently shocking: spaces that resemble prisons (although the European Court of Justice is clear that people who have only been accused of committing an immigration offence should not be incarcerated), no windows, unacceptable beds, food served in plastic bags, no hot water, limited or no access to translation or legal advice, poor or non-existent healthcare and many other complaints. In short, migrants may be treated worse than prisoners, and sometimes in conditions fit at best for animals, which is what detention centres really symbolise – the denial of the humanity of those inside, kept out of view of fellow humans, denied the capacity to act and move, all because they are accused of having crossed arbitrarily created borders.

Open Access Now aimed to make visible this giant injustice, hidden behind a further injustice, which is the denial of our right to know in a democracy how people are being treated using our taxes, in our names. By involving journalists in the campaign, we made allies for the cause of greater public knowledge about the European migration response, and built interest in the plight of migrants. As the situation for migrants has only worsened since 2012, the campaign has morphed into a broader campaign to close the camps, with increasing evidence coming from many organisations and actors of the ineffectiveness and brutality of detention, and its serious psychological effects firstly on the detainees, but also on those running the detention centres.[9]

The rights of man and of the citizen

Why is it that the political response to the migration crisis has been so confused, timid and ineffective? Is it because political leaders are vicious and heartless? Some of them may be, but we do not believe that this is the main reason. Is it because the European institutional structure tends towards the creation of a militarised border to regulate and police mobility? We think this is an important element, fuelled by the non-functional intergovernmental structure of the European Union, among other things. Ultimately, though, this is the *effect* of a civilisational change, rather than the *cause*. Fundamentally, Europe is caught in a dilemma that has deep historical roots, and for which the 'migration crisis' has simply become one of the names and migrants one of the faces. When we look unflinchingly at the human plight of migrants, we cannot justify our own citizenship, and this moral crisis has its political effects, the first of which is nation states trying to deny the problem. It is not a crisis about migrants or asylum seekers but a crisis of citizenship itself, and so we need to look directly at that term. We think that, beyond denial of a problem, there has been an attack on citizenship in recent years, and therefore on meaningful political life, and this has led those whose citizenship is under attack to deny citizenship to others. This war on citizenship is part of the retrenchment of the nation. The way we have been led to think about citizenship is not only inadequate for the migration crisis, keeping us trapped in a schizophrenic situation, but undermines our own political agency. So behind the migration crisis there is really a citizenship crisis, which is one aspect of what we mean by saying that we have become 'citizens of nowhere'.

Let us go back to one of the main origins of the modern conception of citizenship. The Constituent Assembly elected during the French Revolution in 1789 drafted the 'Declaration of the Rights of Man and of the Citizen'. The title itself expresses the uncertainty constitutive of modern citizenship between the universal and the particular.[10] In the declaration, you will not find one set of rights for all men, and one set of rights reserved for citizens: you will find the universal principles that all men are born free and equal in rights, and that the aim of all political association is the preservation of these rights through law. The aspirational, universal side goes along with the particular inscription of rights in law and their guarantee. You will also find the following idea:

The principle of all sovereignty resides essentially in the nation. No body nor individual may exercise any authority which does not proceed directly from the nation.

The nation is both the guarantor of rights and the locus of collective action by citizens to advance their rights. The 'general will' is formulated *as the nation*. But who can be part of that nation? The French Revolution made a radical break in the history of French citizenship by recognising the citizenship of any man who lived in France for a continued period of time. Previously, the bestowal of French subjecthood was reserved for the king, and subjecthood was something that had to be *granted*, not something recognised by the state. At the beginning, the French revolutionaries were more concerned with the class divisions in society than the question of foreigners coming to France, and so debates raged about the citizenship of women, people of colour and those without property. In 1792, the French Republic awarded honorary citizenship to Thomas Paine, Anacharsis Cloots, Joseph Priestley, George Washington, Jeremy Bentham and others, who were nicknamed 'citizens of the world'.[11] This honorary citizenship was the symbolic counterpart to the loss of citizenship imposed on French people who fought against the Republic from abroad. By 1793, though, the foreigner became the image of the enemy. Paine and Cloots, who had been elected to the National Convention, were imprisoned and then sentenced to be executed. Cloots was put to death, and

Paine only got away because a guard had marked the wrong side of his prison door to indicate that he should be taken to the scaffold. But aside from the elites, from 1789 to 1793 hundreds, if not thousands, of foreigners living in France were able to benefit from automatic naturalisation and could become French citizens.[12]

These early years of the French Revolution, which introduced the modern notion of citizenship, show how there was an ongoing set of conflicts and contradictions from the outset regarding which groups have citizenship (women, slaves, the poor) and how much discretion the state should have over who is a citizen (can 'enemies of the state' lose citizenship? What about criminals?), as well as exactly which rights and duties citizenship involves. Much of modern democratic politics has been structured by the struggle over these questions, which are not only legal issues but have social, economic and cultural dimensions.

These questions are all still with us in one way or another and have been supplemented by further queries, but the context in which they are framed has changed, and the political approaches to the struggle that concerns them need to change accordingly. Of course, it is not the first time that this has happened: imperialism and colonialism also changed the structure of struggles over citizenship. The crucial point is that in the contemporary context, articulating the struggle for citizenship exclusively as a struggle over who is a member of the *nation* both limits the emancipatory potential of citizenship and gives the nation a centrality it no longer has.

This is not to say that nation states have disappeared. Rather, they have become one dominant actor among many others in a series of global and regional regimes that govern citizenship. Other actors, which have varying degrees of power and influence, include international courts, international institutions such as the United Nations and Council of Europe, non-national bodies including the European Union, individual lawyers, NGOs and people themselves – citizens and those denied citizenship. Nation states may still be the dominant actors granting, removing and deciding citizenship, but they are not the only ones, and their dominance is being challenged in multiple ways as a complex human rights regime has been developed. Progressive political forces need to take account of this wider transnational landscape of rights, actors and institutions, and act strategically. The reactionary right is certainly doing so.

In the face of this transformation, and the activism of what Theresa May called 'left-wing human rights lawyers' in her October 2016 'citizens of nowhere' speech, one strategy of nation states to reassert their authority has been to promote an understanding of citizenship which makes it something exclusive, a privilege accorded to some but not to others, and always at risk of being taken away. This attack on citizenship has been made using three main strategies: firstly, framing citizenship questions unrelentingly in terms of security, which creates what we call 'disposable citizens'; secondly, a strategic alliance with capitalism to make citizenship a luxury commodity, thereby creating 'luxury citizens'; and thirdly, and most dangerously, by attempting to take democracy hostage through turning foreigners into a threat, which creates what we call 'hostage citizens'. We will discuss each of these kinds of attack in turn, but their combined effect is to undermine citizenship as a form of political agency, and turn it into a mere status of social distinction. As nation states risk losing their monopoly of control over citizens, so they attempt to undermine the radical idea of citizenship itself. This is why it is particularly important not to constrain our vision of citizenship to the national frame.

Disposable citizens

Enough has been written for it to be obvious to everyone that the September 2001 terror attacks on New York were very quickly instrumentalised by all kinds of governments in all kinds of ways: to justify foreign wars, to increase surveillance, to create exceptions to habeas corpus … One aspect of this instrumentalisation that may be less well known is the weakening of citizenship itself. The United Kingdom, and specifically Theresa May when she was Home Secretary, has been a trailblazer in making citizenship conditional, using terrorism as the excuse for doing so. Between 2006 and 2015, the UK Home Office stripped at least fifty-three British citizens of their nationality. In order to do this, the Home Secretary need only be 'satisfied that such deprivation is conducive to the public good'. And since 2014, thanks to legislation pushed by Theresa May, the Home Secretary has been able to denaturalise British citizens even if this renders them stateless – in direct contravention of the 1961 Convention on the Reduction of Statelessness – as long as there are 'reasonable grounds' to believe that the person could *potentially* acquire another citizenship.[13]

While the United Kingdom has been a leader in denationalisation, the idea that citizenship is conditional and can be revoked has gained ground everywhere. It was widely discussed in France following the *Charlie Hebdo* and Bataclan terrorist attacks, and the reform to the French constitution proposed by François Hollande was at one point strongly supported in opinion polls, before being voted down in parliament. Donald Trump regularly suggests that US citizens he dislikes should lose their US citizenship.[14] This line of thinking is the flip side of tests for granting citizenship, but more sinister. If there can be some justification for expecting aspiring citizens to learn about the country they want to become a citizen of, the notion that people should lose citizenship if they are suspected of not matching up to an ideal is a sure-fire route to the government dissolving the people because it dislikes their opinions or actions (and perhaps electing another, in the words of Brecht's famous poem 'The Solution').

Indeed, the recent precedents of such thinking are the worst. The Soviet Union stripped at least 1.5 million people of citizenship. The Nazi regime took care to declare Jews, people with disabilities, Roma and homosexuals illegal before sending them to the death camps. It was with such precedents in mind that the Universal Declaration of Human Rights and the Convention on Statelessness written after the Second World War make it illegal for states to render people stateless.

Without reaching such extremes, the removal of citizenship today is a profound abdication of the state's responsibility for its citizens, as well as an insult to the world in general. Instead of taking responsibility for its own citizens, the state expels them for others to deal with. It is the same 'out of territory, out of mind, out of responsibility' mindset that is applied to refugees. Thus, in the name of security, citizens become disposable, to be jettisoned if they start to cause problems. It does not take much global awareness to see that this is an exceptionally short-sighted way to solve anything.

The expansion in the powers of the state to revoke citizenship leads inexorably to an increase in state control over citizens. While citizenship in its modern formulation originally provided both protection against the sovereign and the capacity for collective action, the discourse of security attempts to remove the absolute protection for all against the government offered by human rights, and makes citizenship discretionary, depending on the will of a government official, court or minister and in the name of the security of the majority. Here, citizenship is made something exclusive rather than universal.

Luxury citizens

Whereas the French revolutionaries awarded honorary citizenship to notable Enlightenment intellectuals, campaigners and politicians for their support of freedom, the trend today is for the selling of citizenship in a global competition for foreign direct investment. The oldest scheme like this is in St Kitts and Nevis and dates from 1984, but there has been a significant increase since the turn of the millennium both in countries offering 'economic citizenship' or residence programmes (a 'golden visa') and in the number of people buying this commodified citizenship. There are estimates that the market in citizenship is worth up to US$7 billion a year, and is increasing rapidly.[15] For a St Kitts and Nevis citizenship, a US$250,000 contribution to the St Kitts and Nevis Sugar Industry Diversification Foundation is sufficient; or, if you prefer, a US$100,000 investment in Dominica will get you a Dominican passport and thereby Commonwealth citizenship. In the EU, Malta offers citizenship for around €1.5 million plus a year's residence in Malta, while Cyprus requires a €2 million property investment, without any residency requirement. Both provide EU and Commonwealth citizenships, and Cyprus is estimated to have made €4 billion since 2014 through such schemes.[16] The UK, the USA, France, Australia, Spain and other powerful and rich countries have similar schemes, albeit with higher fees, and usually more constraining residency conditions.[17]

As with any market, each country has an interest in making its passport the most desirable, and there is a risk that counterfeits or bad product management devalue those passports. Henley and Partners is a law firm in London that describes itself as 'The Global Leader in Residence and Citizenship Planning', and it compiles an annual global league table of the best citizenships to buy, called the 'Quality of Nationality Index'. They also give advice to governments on selling citizenship. Their specialists make breezy comments like 'I've seen more programmes fail than succeed. Belize passports became synonymous with illegal passports'[18] – a comment made as if it did not concern people who did not buy their Belize citizenship but were born with it, a comment made as if it were just a matter of bad investment options. The market may crash, but that is the way it is.

Even if the market does not crash, the sale of citizenship fundamentally undermines the institution of citizenship, forcing us to think of our citizenship not as a political agency but as a commodity which might have a varying price, which may or may not be more luxurious than others, and which, after all, we may lose like any luxury (what could be more of a luxury than something disposable?).

Of course, for the really rich, there remain options even where no formalised sale of citizenship is on the market. Witness the 'honorary' citizenships bestowed on multi-millionaire French actor Gérard Depardieu by Russia and Belgium in 2013 when he disagreed with the 75 per cent tax on the very rich put in place by François Hollande in France. In such ways, the richest always have the possibility of fleeing while the very poorest are priced out of the market, and regular citizens see their citizenship debased as it is transformed into a currency.

Hostage citizens

The most insidious way in which nations have attempted to reassert authority over citizenship is by taking democracy hostage. We encountered earlier the French prosecutor in Nice who called for a severe prison sentence for Pierre-Alain Mannoni. Describing Mannoni's act of driving three young women who needed medical attention across the Italian–French border, he said: 'These actions do not correspond to offering aid, but rather to denying that borders between countries exist and that a country can vote on its laws.' This suggests that, unless a country has sealed borders, its democracy is undermined because it is no longer clear who has a vote. Such an argument puts humanitarian action and democracy in opposing corners, claiming that in order to protect the latter, there must be limits on the former. In the face of an increasingly inter-linked and complex world, the nationalist response is to say: 'In order to preserve our democracy, we need strong borders.' This is the imaginary of the city wall, the policed border of the polis. 'Taking back control' means first and foremost restoring control over who comes into our territory. This is the message most politicians took from the Brexit vote in the UK, and it is the reason why accepting the continuing free movement of people is out of the question for almost all of them.

This argument can be – and regularly is – reinforced by instrumentalising those who are already the most excluded in each country. Robert Fico, the Slovak prime minister, on the occasion of the anniversary celebrations of the Slovak National Uprising, cynically protested against the European Commission plan of quotas of refugees for each member state in the following way:

> After all, let's be honest, we aren't even capable of integrating our own Romani fellow citizens, of whom we have hundreds of thousands. How can we integrate people who are somewhere completely else when it comes to lifestyle and religion?[19]

Already existing discrimination against a minority becomes an argument for not welcoming foreigners, the suggestion being that people who cannot be integrated would simply overwhelm the state and society. Slovakia, a country with a population of around 5.5 million people, was required by the Commission scheme to take a quota of 802 asylum seekers. It is patently ridiculous to suggest that such a number of people might bring a country to its knees.[20]

Aside from the numbers involved, the fundamental problem with such arguments is that they are entirely on the side of state control and state sovereignty, without acknowledging that democratic citizenship is based on a productive tension between the state and the citizens working together politically. Such arguments deny that democracy is about citizens acting together, or that democracy can be performed by citizens acting together irrespective of nationality. In this sense, Mannoni's help in transporting three Eritreans to hospital is political – not an act of charity, but a political act of humanity. The bureau-cratic logic of the nation state is to categorise and divide people: citizen and non-citizen, included and excluded, worker and investor, Roma and non-Roma, young and old. Against this top-down government, the emancipatory logic of the citizenry is egalitarian and non-discriminatory and acts in solidarity. In opposition to the policing of borders, there is the 'solidarity of the governed', to quote Michel Foucault's 1981 speech in Geneva at a press conference in support of Médecins du Monde:

> There exists an international citizenship which as such has its rights and duties, and which is obliged to stand up against all forms of abuse of power, no matter who commits them, no matter who are their victims. After all, we are all governed, and, by that fact, joined in solidarity.[21]

The attempt of the nation state to reassert its authority over people's movement by taking democracy hostage is a way of *promising* a restoration of democratic agency of the citizens, while simultaneously taking away the sources of this civic energy. In reality, what such pledges come down to is the promise of being able to *exclude from the political* – sovereignty is configured as the power to decide who loses their rights. This is the opposite of the power of citizenship to create and act together.

This national top-down thinking leads inexorably to human tragedy on the shores of the European Union, and multiplies administrative and other borders throughout our countries and cities. *Sans papiers* are created everywhere by attempts to police people's access to public services, employment, renting a home, opening a bank account, and so on. Thus, there is a part of the population that is disenfranchised and at greater risk of exploitation. This multiplication of administrative borders and controls leads to a generalised suspicion that is profoundly alienating, preventing us from acting in solidarity as humans. Ultimately, this bureaucratic border state divides and isolates people – either physically by detention or deportation, or by attempting to put a bureaucratic question about someone's nationality and right to residence in the mind of each person offering help to another. In this way, the border state attempts to prevent collective political action – quite the opposite of what the early French revolutionaries may have had in mind regarding sovereignty.

First they came for the Roma

If you take a public bus in Cluj-Napoca, Romania, you could be forgiven for trying to validate a Parisian bus ticket. This is because many of the public buses are old RATP Renault buses that have finished their working life in Paris and have been sold to Cluj. Until quite recently, many of them still had the names of Parisian bus stations and bus routes marked on them, and some even had French number plates. In 2010 and 2011, as European Alternatives expanded its activity further east and opened an office in Cluj-Napoca, this charming experience of déjà vu was complemented by something much more sinister.

In July 2010, Nicolas Sarkozy gave a speech in Grenoble in which he linked together criminality, uncontrolled migration, violence and the Roma. Shortly afterwards, the French government launched a brutal programme of expulsion from France of people identified as living in Roma camps. These actions produced indignation in France and abroad, and, among other reasons relating to the injustice of such racial discrimination, it was pointed out that many of the people concerned had European citizenship, and so had every right to be in France. Viviane Reding, the European Commissioner for Justice at the time, had strong words for Sarkozy's actions, comparing them with mass expulsions in the Second World War. Evidence came to light that the police were carrying out expulsions collectively, and deliberately targeting the Roma, rather than considering each case individually as would be required under European law. Despite the efforts of Reding and many associations, including European Alternatives, the Commission did not stop the expulsions, and the French government led an aggressive advocacy effort to justify its actions. Sarkozy was backed in his condemnation of the language used by Viviane Reding by David Cameron and Angela Merkel, who was herself engaged in expelling Roma from Germany. The powerful President Sarkozy called for compassion for his hurt pride, saying: 'I don't think a European Commissioner is in her role in talking in a way that embarrasses her own colleagues.' Sarkozy himself was comfortable talking in a way that stigmatised some of the most vulnerable people on the continent, and following this up with actions. It was as if European citizenship does not exist.

In Romania – which, like Hungary, the Czech Republic, Slovakia and Bulgaria, has a large Roma population – this affair was followed particularly closely. This was not only because many of the citizens being expelled from France were returned to Romania, but, crucially, because Romania had joined the European Union in 2007 (along with Bulgaria) and had ambitions to join the Schengen area of free movement, and was thus worried that this fuss over Roma would pose obstacles. Bulgaria was keen to blame everything on Romania, and Prime Minister Boyko Borissov assured members of the press that Bulgaria could join Schengen without Romania. 'We are not a federation with Romania and I don't know why we should be examined together,' he protested. Leading Romanian and Bulgarian politicians were emboldened to see that their own game of blaming all problems on the Roma was now being used by the most powerful leaders in the European Union, and so they joined in. In this barbarian rhetoric, Romanian President Traian Băsescu said that Romania considered itself at a disadvantage, because the closeness of 'Romania' and 'Roma' might lead some to think that all Romanians are Roma, which would surely be an insult! One of Băsescu's faithful henchmen, Silviu Prigoană, presented a simple bill to parliament to address this problem: change the official name of the 'Roma', which means 'man' in

Romani, to 'Tigan', which comes from the Greek term for an 'untouchable'.

In Cluj during this time, a project was drawn up to expel Roma living in one of the central streets to a rubbish dump on the outskirts of the city. The area where the rubbish dump is located is called 'Pata Rat', and the fact that living in its vicinity is potentially mortally dangerous is obvious to anyone who might visit. Many of the 300 families living in the area report respiratory illnesses, skin problems and increased cancer rates. Families that had members working and children going to school in the centre of Cluj were expelled from their homes in the cold days of December 2010 and have been unable to return since. European Alternatives, together with local associations Amare Phrala, Desire Foundation and GAS and students and professors from the Babeş-Bolyai University, protested in the streets of Cluj against this action, and have continued to be active. The expulsions from France showed how one part of the population can be treated as expellable, while the parallel actions in Cluj showed how the same population can be treated as disposable. In both cases, there is an attempt to turn men and women from humans into something untouchable, excluded from both politics and the city. These processes have been going on with the Roma for centuries and are a deep stain on any European claim to respect basic human rights. Events since 2010 show how this racism spreads across borders, and how if we do not stand up for the rights of one group, very quickly the rights of every group are brought into question due to the notion of civic rights itself becoming debased. The next bus may be for us.

Citizenship out of the prison

The 'migration crisis' is wrongly named – the crisis is not about migration. There is indeed a crisis, but the crisis is one of citizenship, which means it concerns *us* and our rights, not only the *others*. The movement of people is normal, and unstoppable. The cost of pretending that the movement of people can be stopped is already thousands of lives every year, and rising civilisational panic inside Europe as it becomes patently apparent that this price in blood can only increase. While energy is being expended on the futile project of turning Europe and our countries into fortresses, attention is not being paid to the task of providing citizens, cities and associations with the educational, cultural and financial resources required for a civilisational shift in our understanding of citizenship and solidarity, or in the shape and responsiveness of our political institutions. Addressing the civilisational crisis of citizenship will take time, but some measures, such as those listed below, can be implemented quicker than others.

A humane and effective migration policy

Safe, legal routes for those seeking asylum must be put in place by the European Union, starting with humanitarian corridors for those fleeing war. The European Union must no longer pretend that 'out of sight is out of mind', and that if migrants are not landing on European territory, they are not a European responsibility. If the European Union is capable of sponsoring detention centres outside its territory, it is also capable of running in an orderly fashion asylum processing centres that save those fleeing to safety from having to risk perilous journeys or falling into the hands of traffickers, or worse. Given the difficulty of neatly separating refugees from so-called economic migrants, the same should apply to work visas, with significant yearly allowances of European job-seeking permits made available directly in the country of origin. The only way of curbing the deadly routes of irregular migration is to offer a safe, regular alternative, albeit with a waiting list.

Detention centres are intolerable and must be closed. As an immediate measure, detention centres should be open for journalists and civil society organisations to enter, and the European Union and its member states should set a timetable for the closure of detention centres, with alternatives put in place in terms of reporting requirements of asylum seekers. The detention of children must be stopped immediately.

The Dublin agreement whereby asylum seekers must apply for asylum in the country where they arrive in the European Union is clearly a failure, putting disproportionate responsibility on member states at the borders of the European Union. It should be replaced with a European system that gives asylum seekers agency to move according to family ties, competences and work opportunities in different localities of Europe.

European citizenship

The European Union must ensure equal citizenship for all European citizens whether they are Roma or any other person. The metaphorical bus of discrimination we saw shuttling between France and Romania is ultimately an omnibus that will carry us all unless it is stopped. Any discrimination by member states requires a firm and immediate response; this should include infringement proceedings and the suspension of voting rights at the European Council.

The European Union should ban the sale of citizenship. Citizenship is not a luxury good. If the European Commission does not have competency to do this – something that is disputable, given that, in the words of the Court of Justice, European citizenship is 'destined to become the fundamental status of Europeans' – then member states should act in concert to outlaw this practice. Given that European citizenships are among the most desirable in the world, this move would have global repercussions for the market.

At the same time, the acquisition of European citizenship should be made easier for all those with a genuine link to the continent, whether that be through birth, family or residence. Keeping people in a situation of having fewer rights than their neighbours because of accidents of birth is a racist affront to the egalitarian logics of citizenship and democracy. In the contemporary globalised world, restrictions on dual nationality no longer make sense and act only to exclude people from their rights. All European countries should accept dual nationality.

The European Union should make it impossible to remove citizenship arbitrarily, and not only in scenarios where statelessness would be the result. Citizens are not a disposable good. While there may be some justification for removing citizenship in circumstances of fraudulent acquisition, or in the context of war if a person joins opposing forces, the removal of citizenship should require the utmost judicial oversight, allow the possibility of appeal and be only an exceptional measure.

While the above measures should be taken immediately by European governments and the European Union, the longer-term response to the crisis of citizenship in Europe should be twofold: building the conditions for solidarity on the ground by empowering citizens to act together; and working towards creating flexible and responsive transnational political institutions built on the principle of a right to free movement. The movements of people can be messy, but individual citizens have a remarkable capacity for finding common solutions if they are resourced to do so, as well as for addressing problems through democratic politics rather than through violence. The transformation of the political institutions of democracy in Europe to account for the movement of citizens and their actions across borders will not be achieved in one day, but it must be based on an acknowledgement that neat divisions cannot be made between 'internal' and 'external' politics, of individual countries or of the European Union as a whole, and this means constant democratic dialogue between the European Union and its neighbouring countries, not only at a governmental level but – even more importantly – at a civic level.

Fortresses with clearly delimited boundaries, whether they are cities, countries or continents, give altogether the wrong image. Instead, we should imagine the European Union as a space of translation (etymologically from *crossing sides*), working to build democracy across linguistic, cultural, ethnic and other boundaries. Instead of hiding from the reality of human movement, of all those phenomena that cross and complicate borders and boundaries, the European Union must make all of this *visible, recognisable, human*. Individual citizens need to become translators as well, with the cultural and educational resources to deal confidently with foreignness, to build understanding and collaboration where there may be incomprehension and fear. Providing citizens with these skills requires a significant investment in education and a wholesale reorientation of European policy and discourse, but this is the price of humanising brutal globalisation. We must ensure that the translators, interpreters and those acting in solidarity outnumber the police and the border guards, as a matter of principle, as well as a matter of strategy.

Ultimately, the movement of people is political because it is an expression of our interdependence – it is by its nature an act in relation to others. We need new kinds of political movements, parties and institutions to be able to struggle, discuss and govern in a way that corresponds to this reality, rather than denies it. This is where we turn now.

Chapter 4

Beyond Internationalism: A Transnational Interdependence Party

If socialist parties were active forces, they would have already built a European party, with its policy frameworks, institutions and internal solidarity with a view towards European revolution.

Carlo Rosselli, 1936

Instead of burning committees, set up your own.

Jacek Kuroń, 1970

The power of nobody

Odysseus and his men are washed up on the island of the Cyclops Polyphemus, who eats two of them and traps Odysseus and the others in a cave. The following day he eats two more men, and then goes out grazing his sheep. Returning drunk later in the day, the giant asks Odysseus

159

his name. 'Nobody,' replies the Greek. 'I am called nobody by my mother, father, and all my comrades.' Odysseus has a plot in mind: he stabs Polyphemus in the eye, and when the blinded Polyphemus calls out to his fellow Cyclopes, he says, 'Nobody is hurting me by craft. Force there is none.' His friends laugh and do not come to his aid. In this way, crafty Odysseus gets away, and provides a lesson in how an anonymous nobody can, despite everything, have power. It is a lesson that revolutionaries from Václav Havel (and his famous essay 'The power of the powerless') to Anonymous on the internet have repeated.

In the mid-eighteenth century, in the run-up to the French Revolution, a kind of 'nobody' wrote frequent political publications. This era saw an explosion in the number of pamphlets, tracts and essays presenting projects for universal peace, for a world federation, for a conciliation between the nations of Europe, very frequently published by anonymous authors who would call themselves things like 'citizen of the world', 'friend of humanity' or 'Doctor Man Lover'. Early plans for a European Union were found here, and the most famous of these tracts today is perhaps Immanuel Kant's 'Perpetual peace: a philosophical sketch'. Certainly, one reason for using anonymity was to hide potentially dangerous views from the eyes of kings and their censors, but this is only part of the explanation; indeed, the real identity of the authors was often an open secret. The authors frequently went to theatrical pains to explain that they were just ordinary people, with no particular qualifications, titles or responsibilities – which was obviously false, most ordinary people at the time being incapable of writing literary French or Latin – but the pretence is one that is associated with cosmopolitanism. After all, Diogenes the Cynic, the first 'citizen of the world', presented himself as a mere dog when faced with the mighty Emperor Alexander. In the eighteenth-century Republic of Letters, posing as *nobody* was both a publishing tactic to avoid censorship and an authorial strategy to establish the credibility required to speak on behalf of humanity.

When Michel Foucault spoke in 1981 in Geneva in support of Amnesty, Médecins du Monde and Terre des Hommes – which were mobilising to help the boat people of Vietnam – he also presented himself as nobody:

> We are here only as private individuals and with no other claim to speak, and to speak together, except a certain difficulty we share in enduring what is taking place ... Who asked us to speak? No one, and that is exactly our entitlement ...

This is precisely the grounding behind what he calls 'an international citizenship which has its rights and duties, which is obliged to stand up against all abuses of power, no matter who commits them, no matter who are their victims'. Not only to talk and protest, but to *intervene, to act*. He says that the NGOs have 'created a new right: the right of private individuals to intervene actively and materially in the order of international politics and strategy'.[1] The nobodies, without formal power or privilege, have the right to act on an international scale. This usage of 'international' has come a long way from the origins of the word.

Nationalism and internationalism

The word 'international' was first coined by Jeremy Bentham in 1780, and initially served to replace the expression 'law of nations', which meant the law governing the relations between sovereign states.[2] Bentham was a 'citizen of the world', as named by the French revolutionaries, a correspondent of Mirabeau of the Constituent Assembly, and a friend of the 'Universal Venezuelan' Francisco de Miranda. The latter, after being involved in the American revolutionary wars, had commanded a division of the French army, before being condemned by Robespierre, fleeing to England, then going back to the Americas and establishing the first Venezuelan republic.

As these liaisons suggest, the invention of the word 'international' came in the midst of great political transformations of the word 'nation'. From its early origins in the great Sorbonne University of the thirteenth century, where it indicated 'student nations' by language and origin, the term had gained a political charge that would explode in the French Revolution and in the battles between empires and national independence which would dominate the nineteenth and much of the twentieth century. These were battles over territory and authority, but much more than this they were battle of ideas about how the world should be organised. The 'Declaration of the Rights of Man and of the Citizen' declared the sovereignty of the nation and thereby established the French Republic, but the destiny of this new political form – the republican nation – was undetermined and subject to political struggle. Furthermore, the question of how any given nation related to other nations, empires, the church and all other political actors was new and yet to be discovered.

Entering the world in Genova in the French Empire in 1805, Giuseppe Mazzini was born into this political age of revolutions that would dominate his life and thought. He perhaps encapsulates the figure of the progressive internationalist republican: first in Marseille, then in exile in Switzerland, and then in exile in London, Mazzini promoted national emancipation, founding Young Italy, which spawned Young Poland, Young Germany, even Young France – while at the same time envisaging a 'United States of Europe' as the end goal of his nationalist revolution. His early Europeanism was more than talk – he set up a budding, if short-lived, Switzerland-based international federation to coordinate the struggles: the Young Europe. Mazzini's vision was that of independent, republican nation states – free from the chains of the old regime of empires, secret police and monarchs – that would together create a new European republic based on the free association of free nations. Republican nationalism and internationalism went together. As Mazzini put it:

> Just as without the organization and separation of labor there can be no efficient production, so without

independent Countries there can be no progress of Humanity as a whole. Just as citizens are the individual components of the nation, so nations are the individual components of humanity. Just as every person lives a twofold life, one inward bound and one outward orientated and relational, so does every nation.[3]

Throughout the nineteenth century and until the Second World War, this republican view was common among progressive intellectuals and politicians, from Jean Jaurès to Woodrow Wilson, from Gandhi to Sun Yat-sen. It is important to note that, for most of these people, progressive nationalism was precisely the opposite of xenophobia or warlike national chauvinism. The ordering of the world in nations was instead seen as a way of avoiding aggressive behaviour and of underpinning an international law that would ensure peace. Marcel Mauss, writing after the First World War, put this eloquently in his unfinished and underappreciated study 'The nation':

An internationalism worthy of the name is the opposite of cosmopolitanism. It does not deny the nation but situates it. Inter-nation is the opposite of a-nation. It is in this sense also the opposite of nationalism, which isolates it.[4]

The political meaning of the term 'international' and its relationship with the nation state was never uncontested, however, and Mazzini's was only one view, as the debates of *the* international show.

The International

One of the weak spots of Mazzinian nationalism was spotted early on by another resident of London and a foe of the Italian revolutionary. 'An old ass' is how Karl Marx habitually referred to Mazzini, accusing him of pacifying social conflict by demanding inter-class cooperation to topple Europe's *ancien régime*. The nation, Marx contended, is not the uncontroversial motor of freedom and emancipation that the Italian made of it. Quite the contrary: it can be a fig leaf covering over class differences and exploitation. And while historical progress demanded the surpassing of old empires and the development of a national bourgeoisie, by advocating inter-class cooperation and reconciliation for the purpose of national independence the Italian was entrenching a reactionary system that would keep the people under the yoke of oppression, if only by capital rather than by foreign armies.

International cooperation was key for Marx as it was for Mazzini, but it had to operate along clear class lines. It is perhaps little known that the two men conducted a heated and highly uncertain struggle for hegemony over the foundation of the International Workingmen's Association in 1864, which later came to be known as the 'First International' – a struggle ultimately won by the German in favour of class unity across borders.

The International Workingmen's Association was initially a very European affair: a meeting of German, Italian, French and English workers, in solidarity with Polish workers rising against Russian imperialism. As the nineteenth century progressed, the International developed to include delegates from more and more countries, but divided on different grounds. We cannot tell the full history of the International here, but instead will give snapshots of its divisions through a quick series of three biographical portraits to show how the uncertainties surrounding the meaning of internationalism were lived by some key figures in the movement. The first split, between Marxists and anarchists, was over the roles of parliament and the state and drew on another word that had gained political agency in the eighteenth century: 'federation'.

A federation of what?

Giuseppe Fanelli started his political career in Mazzini's Young Italy, where he fought for national self-determination ... internationally. He was involved in the 1848 first Italian war of independence, in the short-lived Roman Republic of 1849, and then again in 1860 when he joined Garibaldi in his expedition to Sicily. After Italian unification, he went on to fight for the national cause ... in Poland. In 1865 he came back to Italy to be elected in the newly formed national parliament. Soon afterwards, his life and view of the world took a turn when, in 1866, he met Mikhail

Bakunin and decided to switch allegiances from national republicanism to anarchism. Along with Mazzini and Marx, Bakunin was also fighting for hegemony over what would become the First International, and so Fanelli was despatched to Spain to foster the anarchist cause and gain new members for the International Workingmen's Association. Fanelli is considered the first spark that brought anarchism to Spain, where it quickly grew to become the largest anarchist movement in modern Europe.

'If you took the most ardent revolutionary, vested in him absolute power, within a year he would be worse than the Tsar himself.' Bakunin's somewhat prophetic protest against Marxism was a protest against the use of the state to bring about social change. Instead of believing in the dictatorship of the proletariat transforming the state, Bakunin and the anarchists called for society to be reorganised as a federation of collectives, 'with every individual, every association, every region, every nation' having 'the absolute right to self-determination, to associate or not to associate, to ally themselves with whoever they wish'.[5] The word 'federation' itself expresses the idea of free association, consent, agreement or trust, and had become popular among political writers from the mid-eighteenth century, and then especially in the context of the American revolutionary war. Where others called for a federation of states, and some called for a federation of nations, the anarchists called ultimately for a federation of individuals, with each individual free to withdraw from the association if he or she pleases.

The International reloaded

Olga Benário was born in Munich in 1908 to a Jewish family. After joining the Communist Party at age fifteen, she fell in love with an older militant, Otto Braun. When he was arrested and brought to the prison of Moabit in Berlin, Olga arranged for an armed attack to free him. The couple fled to Moscow, where they received political and military training. Olga was then assigned as bodyguard to Brazilian revolutionary Luís Carlos Pestes, with a duty to escort him back to Brazil to foment a revolution. In the meantime, Otto was assigned on the other side of the world to follow the budding Communist Party of China. Olga arrived in Brazil and during the long journey by sea fell in love with the man she was supposed to protect. She went deep into the tropical forest and joined the Brazilian communist insurrection. Meanwhile, Otto arrived in China, where he joined Mao's army and was one of the only foreigners to follow the Chairman throughout the Long March. The insurrection in Brazil failed. Olga was arrested and consigned to the Gestapo. She was deported back to Germany and ended her life in a concentration camp. Otto returned to Moscow, where he spent the war years before being assigned to the newly formed German Democratic Republic.

Just like the revolutionaries of the nineteenth century, a new citizenship of the world was being fostered through political and armed struggle. Its objective, this time, was not the formation of new organic nations but the overthrow of existing, and established, bourgeois state power worldwide.

The Second International, which had been established in Paris in 1889, without the anarchists or trade unions, to follow the work of the First International, discussed again the question of nations and socialist revolution. Where Marx and Engels had been emphatic that socialism in one country was impossible, and the revolution would happen 'at one stroke' as a 'universal revolution' across the world once conditions of economic production were sufficiently developed, their most orthodox followers such as Karl Kautsky moderated this view.[6] Writing on the Social Democratic Party programme adopted in Erfurt in 1891, Kautsky produced a text that was used for decades as an introduction to the political principles of Marxist social democracy.[7] In this text, he argues that once labour exploitation stops, each socialist cooperative, if it is the size of a modern state, will produce enough for its own consumption, and thus international trade will decrease and each economy could be independent except for some 'superfluous' goods. Such a doctrine requires, as Kautsky notes, that each modern state expands to a size where it could be autarchic.

The Second International dissolved at the outbreak of the First World War when the hopes were dashed that the German and French working classes would strike in unity instead of mobilise against each other. Meanwhile, the discussions of the possibility of socialism in one country, which had been a relatively minor concern for the Second

International, became a major concern for one of its partic-
ipants: Vladimir Lenin. The question of whether a socialist
revolution was possible in an economically underdevel-
oped country such as Russia, and whether such a revolution
could survive in the absence of revolutions elsewhere –
notably in major economies such as Germany, France and
England – continued to be major points of disagreement
between the Bolsheviks throughout the Soviet Union.
Whereas Trotsky firstly maintained that through permanent revolution it would be possible for Russia to act as a
vanguard, but only if other countries were pushed to follow
rapidly, Stalin maintained that socialism in one country
was possible, if not complete communism. Ultimately, the
disagreement was lethal for Trotsky, murdered on Stalin's
orders while in exile in Mexico. Olga and Otto's global
peregrinations in the mid-twentieth century occurred in
the midst of these disagreements over the shape and limits
of the socialist international revolution.

The International in the shadows

Ursula Hirschmann was born in Berlin in 1913. In a
section of her remarkable and unfinished autobiography
Noi Senza Patria (*We Without Fatherland*), she narrates how
she cycled with her brother Albert to the headquarters of
the Communist Party in Berlin on 30–31 January 1933,
as Hitler became Chancellor of Germany.[8] Together with
others assembled there in expectation of some response,
they looked towards the top-floor windows of the Karl-

Liebknecht-Haus, where the central committee of the party was deliberating. But no call to action came, and one by one the small crowd disbanded, each leaving in despondency and silence. 'The great red Berlin seemed to be submerged in an unbelievable dream, whilst the hordes of Nazis celebrated their first contact with the drunkenness of power under the windows of the Reichstag,' she writes.[9] However important the role of the Russian Communist forces in the Second World War would turn out to be, for Ursula and others outside the Berlin headquarters that day, their belief in the Communist Party evaporated, well before the horrors of Stalinism came about.

Throughout the month of February 1933, Ursula narrates how the Social Democratic Party held its public meetings, but the orders coming from the party were not to react to the Nazi takeover, not to respond to the provocations of the Fascists. 'Comrades, keep your arms at your feet!' was the order, as the immense crowds left the Sportpalast stadium of Berlin singing the Internationale and the song of the German socialists, 'Brüder, zur Sonne, zur Freiheit' ('Brothers, towards the sun and freedom'). As they left the stadium on the night of 27–28 February, there was a huge number of policemen, and they heard the cry 'The Reichstag is burning!' It was the excuse Hitler needed to suspend the constitution and impose military rule ...

For several more months Ursula and Albert stayed in Berlin, entering the clandestine resistance. Then, when things started to turn particularly dangerous for Jews like the Hirschmanns, they left first for Paris and then Trieste, where Albert finished his doctorate in economics and then volunteered to fight in the Spanish Civil War, and Ursula married Eugenio Colorni and took an active role in the anti-fascist Giustizia e Libertà group, which would result in her being imprisoned by Mussolini with Colorni, Altiero Spinelli and Ernesto Rossi on the island of Ventotene. Out of their discussions on the island emerged the Manifesto of Ventotene, calling for a free and united Europe, which Ursula would smuggle off the island and use to establish the European Federalist Movement. After the murder of Colorni following their escape from the island, Ursula and Altiero married, and while Altiero led federalist efforts in the European Parliament, Ursula militated for gender equality and European unity.

In the opening of her autobiography, Ursula reflects on her life and justifies the title by observing:

> I am not Italian, even if I have Italian children, and I am not German, even if Germany was at some time my fatherland. And I am not even Jewish, even if it is only by accident that I was not stopped and burned in one of the ovens of the extermination camps.[10]

Like many others who survived in the resistance, the only adjective she can live with is 'European'.[11] This activist Europeanism of anti-fascist resistance and solidarity is the forgotten heritage of the European Union.

Beyond anarchy, state and class

However hard-fought the battle might have been between Mazzini, Marx and Bakunin, between international republicanism, socialist internationalism and anarchist federalism in the nineteenth century or between Stalin and Trotsky on 'socialism in one country' in the twentieth century, neoliberal globalisation appears to have finally reconciled these approaches and neutered their radical potential. Firstly, as we have argued repeatedly in previous chapters, neoliberal globalisation is premised precisely on a logic of international, inter-government diplomacy, utilising the myth of nationality to keep populations divided and democracy under blackmail. Secondly, precisely through this process, the 'representatives' of states and governments, as well as leading economic elites, come out transformed into a transnational class separated from any social bond with their nations (the global 1 per cent, which are clearly much more united than the remaining 99 per cent). Thirdly, the state becomes primarily a border-guard agency by which we are all employed, multiplying administrative and legal boundaries throughout its territory in a way that makes the idea of using it as a tool for collective emancipation highly problematic. And lastly, in neoliberalism, the pretence is that each person is on their own, in a market-based competition with everyone else, while it is made practically impossible to subtract oneself from this commerce as our social life itself – as any Facebook user will know – is commoditised. Neoliberalism takes anarchism and monetises it.

The Ventotene Manifesto, written in 1941, understandably sees the chief risk of nationalism being war. It calls for a revolutionary party for Europe to emerge from the ashes of the war, and claims that this party would be *socialist* in having as its goal the emancipation of the working classes and in putting the economy in the service of human flourishing, and *federalist* in that it would unite the nation states of Europe. Yet, against the wishes, warnings and activism of Spinelli, Hirschmann and others, following the Second World War, the nation states of Europe did resurrect themselves, using the European Union as a means and a cover – and this has created a new paradoxical strategic situation: an inter-governmental union that is simultaneously federalised in some of its powers and nationalised in the minds of its population. This combination of undemocratic centralised powers and confined people(s), this 'European archipelago' we explored in Chapter 2 of this book, is a metaphor of neoliberal globalisation, and like good metaphors it simultaneously allows the object of comparison to be seen in a different light and to go beyond this view. Without taking account of this geopolitical and ideological change, many of those today who take up the name of Spinelli – including in the European Parliament, which has his name on the door – willingly or unwillingly act as apologists for the dominance of international capital in neoliberal forms, and empty the vision of those on the island of Ventotene of a socialist society beyond borders of any progressive social content.

Of forums social and unsocial

The structures tasked with governing the new stage of neoliberal globalisation are well known. The institutions emerging from the Bretton Woods era, as we have discussed, have been transformed, with the International Monetary Fund (IMF) and the World Bank becoming the financial firearms for structural adjustment programmes to overhaul emerging economies first and emerged economies later. Just as this process got under way, a loose, global, international forum of leading economies was set up: the G7 emerged in 1975, in the very eye of the storm that would mark the transition from post-war social capitalism to the period of neoliberal hegemony. The World Trade Organization (WTO) was established at one of the peaks of that hegemony, in 1995, and the G20 in 1999, following the Asian and Russian financial crises and the unmasking of the fragility of that hegemony. At the same time, and with increasing pace, new elite gatherings aiming to create an informal forum for steering the world's economy started appearing. The most famous of all, the World Economic Forum, takes place each year in the Swiss resort of Davos, providing a home to the global elite.

These developments triggered a further transformation in international coordination between those refusing the rule of established power – the radical internationalists of our time. Already in the 1960s and 1970s, organisations such as Greenpeace, Amnesty and Médecins du Monde, not to mention the huge Campaign for Nuclear Disarmament movement, gave organisational form to the global awareness of citizens and their urge to intervene directly in the international order. Then the turn of the century, opening with unexpectedly large protests against the WTO summit in Seattle in 1999, was an extraordinarily fertile period of critique of the world that elites were busy celebrating. A genuinely global movement for an alternative globalisation – also called the global justice movement – emerged to raise the alarm on the exploitation of the global South, the pauperisation of increasing parts of the global North, the environmental impossibility of our development model, and the unrestrained and destructive power that international finance was accumulating (tellingly, these are all big issues that, ignored at the time, have re-emerged with a vengeance today).

It is true that the movements critical of globalisation in the 1990s and early 2000s were divided between those calling for no globalisation or anti-globalisation, and those calling for an alternative globalisation. The mainstream media concentrated almost exclusively on the former to present the movement as simply backward. It was the latter, however, that pushed forwards political innovation, refusing to surrender the idea of an alternative world and an alternative globalisation.

It is in this context that a new global citizens' forum first emerged, blending elements of republican internationalism, of the socialist international, and of anarchism. In January 2001, simultaneous with the World Economic

Forum, the first World Social Forum (WSF) was held in the Brazilian city of Porto Alegre. The event exceeded all expectations, bringing together tens of thousands of activists from across the world. With the motto 'Another world is possible', and participation stretching from Latin American peasant groups to European trade unions, from Indian 'untouchables' to African anti-racist movements, the WSF offered a bottom-up, citizen-led alternative to global elite forums.[12]

One of the most widely accepted functions of the WSF was to break the near absolute dominance of the logic of TINA – *there is no alternative*. The idea, in other words, that there was no other model than the neoliberal globalisation that had 'ended history'. For many years the WSF represented the most important attempt at an international coordination of struggles, spawning satellites at all levels of governance: regional, with initiatives such as the Asian or European Social Forum; national, for instance with the Indian or the Italian Social Forum; and even local, such as the Boston or Liverpool Social Forum. It was a whole new dimension of international, multilevel, grassroots political coordination.

While the WSF offered a stupendous counter-power to the discursive hegemony of elite forums, and did much to inform the demands and strategies of the global justice movement, one clear difference with the elite forums was striking: a lack of power. Whereas the WSF offered an open arena for debate and more or less effective coordination between different movements and struggles, the elite gatherings built a loose consensus that directly translated into the formal and informal governance of globalisation.

There is one important lesson here. If you are in a position of exercising agency over the way in which decisions are taken, building consensus allows you to shape policy. If, however, you are at the periphery of politics, as the WSF undoubtedly was, if you are denied a voice in the running of globalisation – if you are a *citizen of nowhere* – then it is not enough to create a consensus among the periphery to speak differently to power. *Changing the world without taking power*, as much as it might be a salutary slogan to draw attention to the ways in which politics is much larger than formal government and institutions, is a slogan for incapacity.[13] Instead, a strategy for *seizing* power, for claiming agency, has to be devised. Even the examples of the far right decisively influencing contemporary politics in Europe from the margins, which we have discussed over the course of this book, are parts of a strategy of the far-right parties to ultimately take power. What is more, the power that is seized needs to be sufficient to affect a systemic change, and that implies also transforming the nature of political power itself, without supposing in advance that it can simply be done away with or ignored.

On all these fronts the WSF fell short. It refused to transform itself into a vehicle for political action to such an extent that Article 6 of its charter expressly barred it from issuing any formal declaration that would 'represent' the position of the forum on any matter. While there were many good reasons for this choice – chief among them the impossibility of reaching consensus and the inherently divisive nature of any representative or voting procedure – this choice undoubtedly hampered the WSF system from creating an effective transnational political actor able to both change the terms of the debate *and* change the resulting policy choices.

This is perhaps best seen in the contradictory position of the European Social Forum. This was a forum that took place in a European Union where a significant degree of monetary, economic and political integration had already been achieved, and where elements of an international proto-government were in place. Europe was crying out for a coordinated, grassroots alternative to that governance, a political insurgency able to enfranchise the continent's citizens; a space capable not so much of 'holding power accountable' as of crafting a political alternative to break the 'divide and rule' strategy of transnational elites and bureaucracies. But this went against the 'open', 'dialogical' nature of the WSF process. And so progressive politics remained in its local and national silos, with at best traditional elements of international coordination, while top-down European governance was being built precisely on the premise that no transnational democratic politics was possible nor desirable.

The result was, in the end, lamentable and highly paradoxical. As the global system and the ideological hegemony that the WSF was born to contest appeared to implode with the 2008 financial crisis, and as Europe entered a period of political and economic turmoil, both the World Social

Forum and the European Social Forum, far from exploiting the new global uncertainty, all but withered away.

The world's colony

If the turn of the century marked the zenith of Western-led globalisation – where one model was put forward as fit for all; where history, following the collapse of Soviet communism, appeared to have ended – today that picture has been torn apart. The snapshot that emerges from global summits today is one of international chaos, with no clear model or hegemon prevailing. For the first time since the break-up of the Soviet Union, a powerful alternative to Western liberal capitalism has re-emerged in the guise of state-led, authoritarian Chinese capitalism (China is aware of it: 'Our country's underlying values hold greater appeal than ever before,'[14] said President Xi Jinping inaugurating his second term in late 2017). Meanwhile, from Russia to Turkey, from Poland to Hungary, an uncanny blend of 'illiberal' democracy and crony capitalism emerges force-fully. The logic of 'There is no alternative' seems to have morphed in a depressing 'There are only bad alternatives'. This disarray multiplies the spaces for neoliberalism to take hold as a global system, but also offers a significant opportunity to introduce a vision for a new politics beyond borders, provided a sufficiently ambitious and innovative political response is offered.

To start to understand the shape this might take, it is useful to contrast the experience of the WSF with similar 'congresses' that transformed global politics. Both the Indian National Congress and the African National Congress began life as forums engaging a plurality of Indian and African representatives in order to craft a common response to colonial rule. Over the first decades of their history, both bodies profoundly transformed their strategy and composition. Slowly but surely, they morphed from forums that aimed to foster dialogue and promote better coordination between their members into political and revolutionary bodies tasked with securing, respectively, national independence from colonial masters in India and full equality for the black population of South Africa.

The turning point for both congresses was the moment of awareness that subjects deprived of political agency have little to gain by crafting common positions in the hope that the *powers that be* will take them up, or even by protesting and campaigning. Instead, it was necessary to construct a counter-power in order to transform a system that structurally deprived colonial subjects of citizenship rights. It was the political, legal, and institutional system itself that had to be revolutionised, not merely certain policies that had to be adjusted. This required a movement that *politically* enfranchised its members through organised struggle in order to legally and institutionally enfranchise the majority who were being denied a voice.

With all due distinctions, we might consider that today's *citizens of nowhere* – notably but not exclusively in the European Union – face a similar challenge. With our autonomy and agency systemically denied, it is no longer sufficient to merely reach a consensus and present alternatives, as many, including ourselves and the experiences we have discussed in this book, have certainly been doing. Nor can we suppose that legal mechanisms alone will give agency to citizens, as if meaningful rights can be 'handed down' from above and not fought for from below. We need an active civic force to struggle for systemic transformation.

As we have suggested in this book, this systemic transformation must simultaneously combat neoliberalism, thereby fighting for human flourishing, dignity and social equality, while responding to the transnational dimensions of our lives and horizons. These are the two legs of the struggle, and we will not be able to move ahead unless we use them both. To be colonised is not only to be disempowered, it is also to be confined, and today's struggle for emancipation, liberty and equality must necessarily go beyond borders.

We began this book narrating the story of Zhang Ying, the Chinese Communist Party official praising democracy for its resilience in times of crisis. We have argued that such resilience resides in the elasticity of democracy, or in its capacity to transform democratic political struggle into real policy change. And we have argued that this elasticity is being lost, in no small part due to the inability of current political systems to operate democratically beyond the limitations and constrictions provided by the inter-national, inter-state regime. National democracies are becoming rigid – increasingly depoliticised, unable to transform demands for change into alternative policy – because no democratic right is truly exercised beyond the narrow boundaries of the nation, thereby hampering the realisation of any genuine vision of a systemic alternative. Without inventing forms of transnational politics, and without contesting, occupying and transforming the already existing institutions of global governance (including national governments) with these forms – in other words, without inventing and enacting transnational democracy – we will not gain the capacity for popular political control over our futures. Instead, we will simply break off parts of the rigidified rubber that previously provided the flex of our democracies, and find that we are left with a broken machine.

To invent the practices and institutions of transnational politics does not demand the federalisation of states, a world government, a United Nations or anything similar. We consider that such ideas focus on the wrong historical actors: nations, states or governments. Proposals like these are trapped in an old 'inter-national' view of the world in which citizens act politically in territorially bounded nation states, and where it is these nation states that are the 'global citizens'. But *citizens today demand the right to intervene directly in the international order*, as Foucault put it; or *citizens today have become transnational in their political horizons*, as we prefer to say. Yet at the same time systemic transformation will not take place without struggle in the political institutions of state and government, and it will not be realised without reshaping and reorganising political power. And so, to turn neo-colonial subjects into full citizens, we propose that we need a new kind of political party, in which citizens act transnationally and actively transform the institutions of government as they do so.

A party with a new worldview

It is easy to forget the basics of what a political party is, so much has the party form been emptied in contemporary electoral politics. The modern political party form was born out of political factions that emerged during the Exclusion crisis and the Glorious Revolution in England, with (very broadly) the Whigs supporting a constitutional monarchy and the Tories supporting an absolute monarchy. The word 'faction' comes from *factionem*, which is *to make or do*, and in Ancient Rome was the term used for teams of competitors in a chariot race. The political factions, then, are groups of people doing politics together for common ideas, competing with other such groups. A political party is precisely that, a *part* of a larger whole; but, of course, different parties may have rather different views about what that whole is. Indeed, having a view of the whole, rather than defending a view of merely a part, is what differentiates a party from a clique or an interest group. The viewpoint is undoubtedly partisan, *partial*, but the gaze is set on the whole community, and the promise – or threat – of transformation embraces all its members.

We are accustomed to seeing political parties operate inside nations: this is the primary 'whole' over which the party has a view. The Whigs had one view of how England should look, while the Tories had another. But even in this nationalised context, the view of *what* territories a country includes, and *who* counts as a citizen of that country – that is to say, the view of what constitutes the whole – can be very different from one party to another. Today, we need transnational political parties to do politics that express different views of what the European and global whole should look like – or, as we might say, with different *worldviews*, but the kind of worldview these transnational parties have would no longer be centred on the nation as the primary actor in world politics. The optics of the way in which a transnational party looks at the world would be different.[15]

Art can offer us a guide. The 'Droste effect' takes its name from the cocoa powder produced by the Dutch brand of that name. In 1904, the artist Jan Misset produced a very particular design for the tin containing the powder, which portrayed a maid holding in her hand the very same tin of cocoa, including the same image of the same maid holding the same tin box, which in turn obviously featured an image of the maid holding the tin … and so on, theoretically to infinity (but practically as far as the resolution of the image allowed). The idea of a picture within a picture is not new: it goes back at least as far as Giotto, who in the fourteenth century crafted a triptych that contained the image of Cardinal Stefaneschi offering the very same triptych to Saint Peter. In literature, this would become the 'play within a play within a play' that Shakespeare was so fond of.

A similar effect dominates our understanding of political interdependency today. As globalisation appears increasingly out of our control, prey to forces we cannot influence, and as the European Union seems to turn into a rule of all against all where only the interests of the strongest prevail, our reaction is often to recoil and attempt a return to a smaller unit, one that we feel might still listen to our concerns. Put simply, to a bordered nation in which we might still hope to 'take back control'. Caught within this disorderly international order, however, our nations themselves are increasingly unable to guarantee such control. If the lack of agency at a transnational level is blatant, the reduction of democratic choice within the nation is equally so, as we have shown in the first chapter of this book, referring to the broken clock of Western democracy. Some react to this situation by demanding 'more nation', which usually translates into a race for higher border walls and an increasingly exclusionary conception of who 'belongs' within that nation. Others respond to the incapacity of the nation state to protect – to fulfil what we described as Polanyi's second movement – by attempting to deepen regional autonomy or demand the formation of newly independent, smaller nations, in the hope that a reduced scale (and, for some, a more ethnically homogeneous nation) might facilitate 'control' over state politics. Some see in the smaller scale of the city the possibilities for greater democratic control: think of the emancipatory new municipal movements in Spain. The trend does not necessarily end here. Inspired by, among others, the confederal model of Rojava in Syria, some demand greater empowerment for neighbourhood assemblies and a system of confederation between such assemblies.

Let there be no mistake – bringing democracy as close as possible to citizens is a worthwhile and necessary endeavour. However, *on its own*, the drive to a smaller scale will not produce any significantly greater empowerment or enfranchisement, as all these political units are subject to mutual interdependency. Take the example of economic policy, something that is most glaring within the Eurozone. The dysfunctional set-up of the common currency area – the lack of common investment or fiscal union, for instance – drastically constrains the room for manoeuvre for nation states. The lack of a transnational democracy able to steer the Eurozone in the interests of a majority of its citizens means that national citizens see their options reduced, as countries strive to comply with budget constraints within an obtuse economic framework in which they have little agency. This, in turn, has an impact on the freedom of manoeuvre of municipalities, which see their funding reduced, any surplus redirected to covering the central budget deficit, and reduced capacity for investment. Which, finally, limits the scope of any innovation that a neighbourhood assembly might want to bring to a particular area.

Several more examples could be provided, from climate change to managing migration flows. The point is that, from the global to the very local, democracy and agency rise or fall together. Recuperating control over transnational politics implies at the very same time increasing the space for agency offered at regional, municipal or neighbourhood scales. For these are not separate, watertight containers, but different instances of a single movement: politics.[16] Our objective should be recuperating political agency over this continuum, developing a vision for the whole and a political practice able to cross its boundaries. In this fragmented and fractal situation of global governance, in which neoliberalism profits by exploiting the disjunctures of the system, political action needs to take place in multiple arenas, facing multiple authorities, and in multiple countries and contexts if it is to have a chance of bringing real change.

We began this book by narrating the myth of Europa in order to remind us that in its original conception Europe refused to be delimited and bordered, but was to be found in movement and transition. This is also our understanding of politics. The challenge we have in front of us is that of creating new political institutions and practices that can operate across such uninterrupted movement. By traversing levels of governance that the hierarchical nation-state vision of the world would keep separate, Europe as an idea both challenges territorial borders and reconfigures the looking glass through which we view politics, forcing us to see simultaneously both the inside and the outside of any group we constitute.[17] Whereas the national world is configured as a world of Russian dolls, with nations containing regions, containing cities, containing individuals; where the optics of the inter-national world are those of the Droste effect, where the same bordered spaces reappear infinitely at every level and present an inescapable prison; the transnational vision of the world is one of the *moebius strip*, a continuum where the outside is folded into the inside and vice versa. Transnational political parties would take a step outside the frame of nationalised politics by taking transnational citizens as their focus. This means that the party would have in view citizens who should have the power, resources and liberty to move and to act collectively as equals. Such citizens would no longer be citizens of nowhere in the negative sense, but would be citizens of the world with the agency to create, recreate and pursue utopia.

The European Union, due to the particularities of its already existing transnational institutional structure, the centrality of free movement to its principles, and the 'global' impact of any significant changes to such a key economic area of the world, offers a good starting point to begin practising a new conception of politics beyond borders. But whatever peculiarities the European space might have, and however we might translate these into a particularly *European* political response, such a strategy will make sense only to the extent that it perceives itself as a partial movement within a general attempt at building a democracy that questions all delimitation of political space.

Who does the party belong to?

It is a frequently made objection that there can be no democracy in Europe because there is no European *people*, no European *demos*. This objection can obviously also be extended to other geographical regions. There are various things that this objection may mean, but our basic answer to all of them is this: for a democracy, you do not need a people, you need parties!

The idea that a 'people' is required for democracy to be possible is often tied up with the idea that democracy can only take place in a unitary space, where a sovereign authority is supposed to be in more or less complete control of the laws affecting that space – and then the question becomes to what extent the sovereign is representative of the people. This vision of politics has never been more false: our lives are governed by multiple and often competing authorities, and the spaces we live in are thoroughly intertwined in such a way that events very far away may have immediate repercussions nearby.

What would hold such parties together, if not common belonging? The examples of the Indian and African National Congresses we have already mentioned are useful to distinguish two forms of solidarity that are usually confused in colonial settings, for there are two ways of expressing the anticolonial struggle. One way would be to say that they were the parties of struggle for blacks or (ethnic) Indians in South Africa or colonial India; another would be to say that they were the struggle of all those oppressed by the colonial powers. Of course, in these cases, the two things went largely together, but there is no need for this always to be the case. A party can be based around the solidarity of the oppressed, and can have as its mission the desire to bring the oppressed to see the commonality of their condition and the need to struggle together to overcome it. 'Intersectionality' has become a guiding word for the way in which the political struggles for gender equality, LGBTI rights, anti-racism and other fights against discrimination intersect. We need a political party that is both intersectional and transnational as it takes as its highest oppressor the global neoliberal regime and its ensuing disenfranchisement of all citizens.

If a 'party' is simply understood as a group of people doing politics and driven by similar ideas, then this party already has significant force. For there is already a large worldwide ecosystem of organisations and individuals working to fight neoliberalism, for free movement and for progressive global politics. We have given examples throughout this book of how 'another Europe' of civic action exists and is well ahead of the formal institutions. But this group does not express or understand itself as a *party* with a worldview and the will and organisation to drive it through, whether in Europe or across the world. It exists in *potentiality*, but rarely acts on that potentiality, and never for very long.

Still, while it is important not to underestimate the number of adherents a new party potentially has and the need to which it is responding, there is no hiding the fact that the citizens currently thinking in these terms are a small minority. What is more, the citizens who are most likely to join and support such a party in the short term are likely to come from the more or less privileged younger generations and educated middle classes, who may be facing precarity, lack of affordable housing and a whole series of other problems, but are probably not the 'working class'. How is it possible to create a party that would call itself progressive if it forgets about the working class, or about rural populations, or about the poorest in society in general, it might be asked? These objections have force given the alarming tendency in recent protests in Romania and elsewhere for 'the beautiful people' to criticise the 'backward' classes who have voted for the current governments.[18] A certain middle-class scorn for the 'stupidity' or lack of education of anyone who may have voted for Brexit in the UK, or for Trump in the US, is a familiar and similar phenomenon.

We have two responses to this criticism. Firstly, it is a patronising and abusive generalisation to suppose that less educated or less wealthy people are *automatically* nationalist, reactionary, racist or backward, or indeed to make the generalisation that somehow *all* the working class voted for Brexit or Trump or whatever. This is demonstrably false, and attempts to define the 'working class' working backwards from those who voted for Trump or Brexit, rather than the other way around. Secondly, and more importantly, a political party needs to conceive of its task as persuading others of its views, because it believes in a vision of a good world, a good society and a good politics. The creation of political parties should not be based on opinion polls, but rather on substantive ideas and a desire to influence opinion. There are very strong arguments that neoliberalism and nationalism are particularly bad for those lower on the income ladder or with lower levels of education, and extremely disadvantageous for rural populations and those outside metropolises, so these arguments need to be made publicly in discussion with those who may not currently be thinking of them – and, of course, without condescension, which defeats any attempt at persuasion. It is a highly simplistic political sociology to suppose that there is some predefined group called the 'working class', which is represented by progressive parties. Rather, the purpose of progressive political parties has always been to persuade people that they are part of a group, because they must struggle together to improve their condition through common coordinated strategies. Thus, while it is true that progressive political parties must not forget about or ignore the weakest in society, it is no argument against the formation or existence of progressive political parties that the weakest or most disempowered in society do not *already* agree with them. Political education, ideological critique, debate and discussion have always been vitally important elements of the strategy of progressive political parties. These points are straightforward, but we believe that the role of genuine political parties has been so debased in recent years that it is necessary to remind ourselves of them.

It should also go without saying that a transnational interdependence party would not limit its membership by nationality. Although – as we will discuss below – we think that the European Union presents particularly auspicious conditions for creating a transnational political party, such a party would not consider itself 'European' in its membership or identity. It would not be a party that 'belongs to' the Europeans, as if the Europeans were a distinct 'people'. Rather, membership would be open to anyone from anywhere, including other organised political forces, trade unions, civil society platforms and social movements wishing to engage in an innovative experiment of transnational political coordination. The party would have different strategies for the different authorities and state institutions it seeks to address and influence. The EU bodies would be one such set of institutions with their own geography, but so would the Council of Europe, national governments, local governments, the United Nations, international courts and so on. The party would not be defined by the institutions it seeks to influence or infiltrate, and it would not be defined by territorial borders. As such, it 'belongs' to no one in particular, or to all citizens of nowhere.

A party beyond and between the institutions

One consequence of a political party setting its focus on transnational citizens is that it would be placed simultaneously beyond and between formal institutions of state and politics. The party would care for all the ways in which politics is conducted outside the institutions, and would also see the limits of any one formal political institution in 'representing' citizens. Since there is no possibility (or desirability) of a global parliament that includes everyone, any individual formal political institution will inevitably be limited and create exclusions. Therefore, the party will consistently act within and between several institutions.

As a result, going beyond the nation state also involves going beyond representative democracy. Let us go into more detail about each of the main ways in which the party would act beyond and between institutions.

Opinion forming and re-forming

We have already emphasised throughout the book that parties should be active forces capable of playing a central role in directing arguments, disrupting and transforming the space of what is possible and imaginable. At the moment, the parties of the far right do this much better than progressive parties, but there are examples from the progressive side of politics that can serve as inspiration. If we look at events since the 15-M or '*Indignados*' wave of protests in 2011, Spain provides many such experiences. The extraordinary social mobilisation of recent years mainstreamed positions that had generally been relegated to the periphery of public debate, from participatory democracy to regulation of the gig economy and platforms such as Airbnb, from feminism to the discourse on the commons. As the wave of the protests subsidised, the new political forces directly emerging from such experiences – such as Podemos, the '*mareas*', and Barcelona en Comú – have played a significant role in maintaining these issues high up the agenda and promoting political and discursive fights that aim to transform them into new common sense.

A transnational political party would be even more ambitious, notably in elevating awareness of the implications of 'local' decisions on more distant populations. This is something that is already increasingly common when it comes to environmental concerns, as green groups and parties have been effective in explaining that pollution produced locally, or resource extraction, may have potentially catastrophic knock-on effects in another part of the world. 'Externalities' are increasingly self-evident when there are limited natural resources: the number of fish in the sea, for example, is limited, and so any one group overfishing has an impact on everyone else (and rapidly, of course, on the group overfishing, which is why nationalism in fishing policy is absurd). In other areas of politics, such externalities are less immediately obvious to us, but in recent years they have been increasingly damaging in the economic sphere in particular. The damage that can be caused in neighbouring countries by a mercantilist policy of large trade surpluses, for example, may be obvious to economists, but in political discourse this has often been translated as '*we* are virtuous savers, and *they* are profligate spenders, and so our advantages are justified!' A transnational party would counteract such moralising politics by structurally undermining the difference between 'us' and 'them'. It would, for instance, campaign forcefully in Germany to explain why fiscal solidarity and the democratisation of European economic policy would not be tantamount to charity from the north to the south, but would rather constitute a building block for a fairer society all across Europe – including in Germany.

Empowering civil society

A transnational party – in the way we understand it – should be a new kind of entity capable of giving voice to citizens and strengthening social dynamics, and not a mere collector of votes and seats. Most political parties that are successful in entering political institutions become rapidly dominated by their parliamentary or institutional wings. The transnational party in parliament(s) should serve the wider transnational movement outside the institutions, not the other way round. Although no political party can be immune to this danger, a transnational political party will be structurally more protected from it by the fact that it does not aim to take power in any particular governmental institution, and so any governmental power it does manage to win will be partial with respect to the breadth of the party. A national political party that wins national power, on the other hand, risks being totally subsumed by the national government.

Over the course of this book we have argued that there already exists a lively ecosystem of citizens and civil society organisations calling for a new system. This is what we have termed the 'fast lane' of citizens. But while episodic movements, citizens' platforms, NGOs and activist organisations exist, they don't have any meaningful organisation, or political representation, beyond the speci-ficity of their own work or concern. This is not just about institutional representation – a seat at the table. It is about lacking organisation that maximises the impact of diffused

actions for systemic change: through resource management and allocation (particularly to move resources from
centres towards peripheries), or through the formation of
joint messages and joint strategies oriented relentlessly to
taking, using and reforming power. A sustained organisation of civic energies is all the more important given our
task: shaping a new capacity for doing politics beyond
borders. And so it will not be enough to simply foster *more
of the same*: that is, more effective civil society actions, with
better structure, better organisation. We need to foster the
capacity for individual struggles, practices of activism and
citizens' participation to develop a transnational perspec-
tive and horizon of action.

To be blunt, we need to move beyond the naivety of
swarms and multitudes, the idea that the spontaneous acti-
vation of citizens is sufficient on its own to drive politics
forwards. The naivety of this position is to think that
without structured organisations the processes of learning,
of coordination and of the stewardship of resources
can happen automatically. And, furthermore, without a
common organisation between activists, it is not clear that
their strategising for action relates to the entity as a whole
and not to each of them individually: it is one thing to think
about what you should do to promote a fairer world, but it
is another to think about what an organisation as a whole
should do, and what your individual role in that might be.
And where there is an organisation, there are necessarily
hierarchies in the sense of people taking greater responsibility for some organisational functions and concerns

than others. Rather than pretending that these hierarchies do not exist, we should make organisations that are democratic, in which those in positions of responsibility are accountable and removable. Only then will we have parties that are independent of their leaders and do not risk becoming personality cults.

While the party would be an avant-garde in the sense of providing a vehicle for transformation, it would not be an avant-garde in the sense of being a handful of 'enlightened' leaders seeking to lead the people to freedom. Instead, the party would be a space of coordination and collaboration, and its main objective would be to multiply civic energy by creating and maintaining connections, with a view to building, taking and transforming power. As anyone who has been involved in creative collective processes knows, the most productive collaborations are usually those where there is some degree of tension and difference in approach between collaborators, but where this tension is channelled into the process and the output. Our vision of a transnational interdependence party is of a space that can bring together different actors committed to a similar vision of a desirable world, but with different contexts and approaches, in a highly fruitful and productive process of co-creation.

Historical continuity

The work of a transnational party would take place over time – it is not just about organising a protest or a strike but developing a continuity of action. This is all the more important where the action of the party spans different geographical contexts, different thematic concerns and different kinds of action. This could include legal activism in the courts, citizen organising in neighbourhoods, citizen mobilisation in the streets, media activism, artistic activism to break out of the neoliberal prisons of our minds, and action through parliaments. As these examples suggest, the actors in this new politics are highly varied: lawyers, citizens, artists, refugees, politicians, journalists and so on. A transnational interdependence party would seek to coordinate this activity, to articulate shared objectives and horizons of action, and to provide continuity to the work over time and space through education and knowledge transfer and by articulating a history of common struggle. Although it would act in formal political arenas such as parliaments, which are potentially hugely influential places of power that can turn into vast obstacles for progressives if they are abandoned to the right, the party would not fetishise this form of governmental power from above, which is only one element among an array of practices and locations that produce politics.

Beyond holding together and coordinating the different actions of the party and allowing for learning, there is a deeper reason why the question of time and continuity is essential for the transnational party. We started this book with reference to the utopias of the nineteenth century, those of Bellamy, Morris and others. What is striking with these utopias is that political time has come to an end: in the utopia, politics has been solved after the best and most just organisation of the people has finally been found. Our utopias today cannot pretend that history will come to an end, or that at some point politics will no longer be necessary. We think that there will always be the possibility of humans grouping themselves in exclusive ways, of inequalities emerging and being exploited, and of events changing historical circumstances in unexpected ways. History is open-ended, and politics must be too. Thus, the transnational party sees itself as endlessly working to undo closed groups, to struggle for equality and dignity and to invent new political forms. This open-ended history allows the transnational party also to offer an interpretation of past history, to find, re-find and reinterpret its historical roots and predecessors, and to reclaim from history its radicality.

The incompleteness of any institution

Since any political institution that needs to take decisions, whether it be a parliament, a law court or a public treasury, will inevitably only have a partial view of a global common good, no institution can be fully representative. Aware of this fact, the transnational party will have to work in multiple institutions, not seeking to make an impossible monster global state, but rather to struggle in multiple locations to promote equality and progress, and to use the diversity of institutions in a virtuous way as a system of counterpowers and balances, rather than allow them to be exploited as a way of dividing and disempowering the citizen.

There are strong arguments for multiplying institutions and creating new transnational chambers. Benjamin Barber has argued for a parliament of mayors to build on the leading role that cities have been playing in addressing climate change and social segregation, in welcoming migrants of all kinds and in other areas.[19] European Alternatives, linking up with initiatives led by cities such as Barcelona, has been making its own mapping and networking of such municipal practices throughout Europe.[20] What is clear is that cities are at once highly inventive spaces for the implication of citizens in governance, and limited in how much they can achieve if they are not networked and are unable to build counter-powers of scale to national governments. A parliament of mayors or a radical transformation of the Committee of the Regions, which already exists inside the EU institutions, could therefore provide an energising and inventive new body, able to work on different geographical scales compared with any existing institutions, and able to involve citizens in unprecedented ways.

At the same time, the march of the transnational party would not leave existing political institutions untouched. Quite the opposite – it would radically challenge all political institutions that are premised on closure and borders, and seek to subvert them by bringing the point of view of the outside inside. In November 2017, theatre director Milo Rau organised a general assembly in Berlin, inviting representatives of civil society and political movements from across the world to have a say in the Bundestag, the German parliament. The argument was simple: German policy impacts the whole world, but the whole world has no say over it.

Imagine a transnational party that competed for government in a national context, but welcomed the input of people from other countries into its programme: in this way, it would bring the excluded into the national parliament and subvert the limits of this institution. Imagine a party in the European Parliament that brought into its deliberations on the desirability of a trade deal between the European Union and India individual and civil society members of its party from India to discuss how they saw its advantages and disadvantages. Beyond campaigning *against* trade treaties prepared from above, it would have the resources to present alternative treaty solutions prepared by all sides concerned. Imagine, again, a party that were able to bring together members from Europe and Africa to devise a joint programme for the management of migration flows. Or, finally, a party that, if the United Kingdom does leave the European Union, includes members from both entities in its deliberations when it comes to issues that touch on the relationships between the EU and the UK, or decisions that indirectly concern both.

A disobedient party

The idea that without conflict and constant insubordination the status quo is detrimental to the interests of the majority is a historical pillar of democracy. In the institutions of ancient Republican Rome, according to Machiavelli, conflict was not merely a temporary disruption of order; it was rather the very matrix of the body politic and the political dynamic that both emerged from and ensured the continuation of the spirit of liberty.

From 453 BC onwards, the Roman lower classes developed a peculiar way of addressing their civic anger: they would occasionally evacuate the city and encamp on a nearby hill. 'They kept themselves for several days, neither being attacked, nor attacking others,'[21] wrote the historian Titus Livius (Livy). This secession was nothing more than an appeal for the re-foundation of the political community. As Livy indicates, the plebs agreed to return to the city only when the senators succeeded in fashioning a narrative that recognised the plebs' significance to society. The institution of the Tribune of the Plebs – the ones who had the power to veto the decisions of the Senate – was born out of these secessions.

Partisan conflict is, in this sense, often necessarily *unlawful*, to the extent that it aims not merely to redistribute goods within a given order, but to question the very institutions of that order and to demand their renewal. The history of modern struggles for democracy and liberty is, after all, often the story of *illegal* acts that are profoundly just: from the expansion of the franchise we mentioned early on in this book to the extension of voting and civil rights to women, from the freedom of colonial subjects to the full equality of black people living in the USA or South Africa. This is why each and every status quo, seen with the eyes of the future, must appear unjust and exploitative.

Modern democracy is premised on historical change, one that often outpaces and triggers the transformation of the legal and institutional framework.

A significant aspect of the attempts to de-politicise democracy over the recent past is precisely its reduction to a system of retribution and redistribution, where different actors merely compete for access to limited resources. But today we need parties that are able to demand a transformation of our political institutions and constitutions, parties with a worldview that includes changing the world system. This may call for an array of disobedient acts, including civil disobedience on the streets and institutional disobedience in the parliaments. Imagine, for instance, a party able to coordinate the disruption of parliamentary work across Europe to resist the implementation of the scandalous EU–Turkey deal on refugees, while at the same time working with civic activists to block repatriations of refugees. Referencing our narrative on the plights of Cédric Herrou and Pierre-Alain Mannoni, we would need a party of men and women able to filibuster the French and Italian parliaments in the morning and aid migrants to cross the border – and, if necessary, face public arrest – in the afternoon.

Or, similarly, take the paradoxical position of a city such as Barcelona. A large 'Refugees welcome' banner hangs outside City Hall, and provisions have already been made to provide housing to refugees relocated from other European countries. The central Spanish government, however, has blocked most such relocations. A transnational party would work with city administrators and movements to autonomously organise a relocation, say from Palermo to Barcelona. This would potentially imply violating Spanish law while, interestingly, respecting the European directive on relocations at the same time. It is also by triggering institutional crises such as this that democracy – and humanity – advances.

Starting in Europe

In this book we have attacked inter-governmental, inter-state Europe, the system pitting nation against nation in a process in which only the most powerful national oligarchies prevail and the common interest of the majority of citizens is crushed. The absence of real democracy in European decision making is a platitude by now. But there is at least one other democratic deficit to confront: the difficulty of political society to organise itself transnationally. While we demand democratic *institutions*, Europe still lacks effective democratic *practices*. And this depends largely on us.

The European Union presents considerable opportunities for creating new transnational political forces and practices, and perhaps greater opportunities than in other parts of the world. This is partly because the European institutions have an evident transnational dimension, and therefore can be the ready focus of political energies beyond the nation state. Just as importantly, free movement and free legal establishment inside the Schengen area and the single market offer considerable and largely unexploited opportunities for creating political movements beyond borders. In creating European Alternatives over ten years, we have been surprised that few other civic organisations have taken advantage of the possibilities for a *single organisation* to employ people and be active throughout the European Union: typically, civil society organisations still work in partnership with local actors when they work outside their 'home' country, but we would argue that this model of 'international cooperation' is outdated.

The European Parliament should be a leading institution for democratising global governance and developing politics beyond the nation state. Since the Lisbon Treaty, the European Parliament has had considerable power over most European Union legislation, having what is called 'co-decision' with the European Council, and it has what should be a powerful veto over trade deals made with countries outside the EU. And yet to many it appears simply as the crown on the head of an undemocratic intergovernmental federation. If the European Parliament is often bypassed when it comes to the most important decisions made over European politics (witness the Fiscal Compact, which was made outside the community decision-making procedure) or is impotent to substantially influence European decision making early in the process (witness the failure of the European Parliament to weigh in substantially on TTIP or CETA[22] before the latter was vetoed by the tiny regional parliament of Wallonia), this is partly because of the dominance of conservative forces in the parliament and their connivance with national leaders from the right-wing political family, but substantially because the European Parliament is filled with politicians who have only a derivative relationship with party politics and lack any rooting beyond the institutional dimension. Without real European parties, the deliberations of the European Parliament are totally detached from political forces outside the institutions. Without real connection with citizens and movements, existing parties cannot call on citizens to reinforce their hand in acts of defiance, such as censoring a trade agreement or paralysing the EU budget in protest. The politicians themselves often put the blame on the media, and in Brussels there are endless – and largely fruitless – conferences on how to make the media more interested in the activities of the European Parliament, as if public interest could be decreed from above. The problem is not the media: it is the form of politics in the parliament.

European political parties exist only in name; in reality they are neither *European* nor *parties*. Inside the European Parliament, the members sit in political groupings that have been created by bringing together the representatives of more or less similar national political parties. These umbrella groupings may vote more or less coherently on 'party' lines, but they function very much in the same way as the European Council, with national party representatives negotiating to agree on a common line. They are inter-national and not transnational. The European elections are not European, but rather a series of national elections, of representatives of national parties that may or may not flag up their European grouping. Recently, a legal form for European political parties and foundations has been created, but this form is again one of a federation of national parties, not of genuinely transnational European parties. As a form, it has been used only by the European groupings already represented inside parliament, as a way of accessing funding from European budgets. Such a system is Europeanism designed from above on an international model, and not the result of European political forces being built by citizens. The political 'parties' that result from such engineering do not have any popular anchoring in social struggle, and are constitutively distant from citizens and real politics.

While expecting that European democracy will come from the designs of international powers is a pipe dream, there is space and an overwhelming need for European democracy to be created by the citizens, organising themselves into new parties with a view to infiltrating the European Parliament and transforming the use made of its formal powers. If transnational politics can be shown to be a success inside the European Union, this will provide a bridgehead for a budding transnational party from which an assault can be launched on neoliberal governance in other arenas.

We have argued that, while a transnational party will not prioritise governmental power or formal institutions above other forms of political power, it will use all opportunities to gain power and change the direction of politics. In this sense, the European elections present a significant occasion to bring civic energy back to the European project, and for political invention that is about more than just winning seats: they are an opportunity to create a force and a political insurgency that can empower us as citizens of the world. The European Parliament, which is not prioritised by the current common sense and nationalised worldviews, could become the fulcrum of a transformation in the meaning of our citizenship and political agency, if we organise politically to use it in this way.

A constituent assembly for Europe: a proposal

Waiting for European democratic reform to happen is more frustrating than waiting for Godot. In the Beckett play, Godot is clearly never coming, and at least in the eternal wait we can meditate on the absurdity of human existence (and anyway the play will finish at some point). In the European Union, democratic reforms are coming at some point, but are seemingly endlessly deferred, and when they do come, it is highly likely that as a result of political compromise and national obstructionism they won't be what is needed. In the meantime, for lack of ambitious European democracy, the forces of reaction and nationalism grow, so that, on the one hand, democratic reform becomes less likely, and, on the other, any such reform is less likely to be satisfactory or ambitious. A perfectly vicious circle.

It is time to stop waiting for others. Godot isn't coming. We have argued that European elections can be an important moment to mobilise citizens around the request for democratic change, but change will not come through the official ballot boxes alone. And so, in addition to fighting in the official elections and getting votes in the official ballot boxes, citizens need to set up their own ballot boxes, and even their own elections.

We can envisage the transnational party working to 'hack' the European elections as an act of civic disobedience that will open up alternatives. The occasion could be used not merely to *demand* but to *elect* a constituent assembly for Europe tasked with drafting a democratic constitution for the EU. Between 1956 and 1963 Altiero Spinelli organised regular transnational elections to appoint a 'Congress of European people', a prototype constituent assembly for a federal Europe. Elections were organised by volunteers, with citizens invited to vote in physical booths from Turin to Vienna. In the era of digital participation the idea could very well be taken and scaled up.

This political and performative act would work as follows. All candidates in the official European parliamentary elections, as well as all citizens, NGOs, social movements and any individual who declares an interest in the future of Europe, would be able to stand for the constituent assembly. These candidates may organise themselves in transnational lists, and European parties would be directly asked to field candidates for election, so as to create an immediate link between the emerging assembly and the European Parliament. On the day of the elections, in as many cities, towns and villages as possible across Europe, outside the official polling stations, there would be the possibility to physically elect members of the constituent assembly. Elections would be simultaneously held online. As a result of these elections, which should be accompanied by as much publicity as possible, a group of several hundred elected representatives would have been chosen.

Following the elections, the assembly would meet as the elected representatives together with citizens selected at random (via sortition) and interested groups to elaborate ideas for the values and contents of a democratic European constitution. Online, a wiki-constitution would be discussed and drafted collaboratively. Indeed, the assembly would be a significant actor in initiating a wider process of citizens' assemblies, through a cycle of meetings, discussions and debates organised in town halls, schools, universities, cultural spaces and other local venues throughout Europe, with coordination and exchange between these different cities and citizens.

The idea would not be that the constituent assembly itself would have the legitimacy to decide on a new constitution. Rather, the assembly would serve as a new civic power to inject ideas for democratic renewal into the European institutions and ensure that they cannot be ignored or sidelined in any future convention or treaty change – an affair normally reserved for national elites and their bureaucracies. The assembly could be accompanied by a secretariat and would operate as a new kind of organisation: between a citizen-led NGO and a democratically elected congress. It would, to an extent, hark back to the experience of the national congresses we have described above. Ultimately, we think creative acts of disobedience and invention such as these are a way for citizens to gain agency in international processes and open transnational spaces for alternatives.

Citizens of Nowhere:
A Rallying Cry

This book takes its title from a phrase uttered by Theresa May after the UK voted to leave the European Union: 'If you believe you are a citizen of the world, you are a citizen of nowhere.' We have reversed this phrase to argue that we are all already citizens of the world, but until we invent forms of politics beyond borders, we will remain citizens of nowhere, without political agency. The utopia we have presented in this book is one of transnational citizens, living and acting across borders, who have the agency and resources to move freely, who have the power to work together as equals, who constantly invent new strategies for ensuring their autonomy to live rich, meaningful lives together, and who continuously struggle together for a better future. This is a vision we think is realistic for all citizens, not just an elite few, and we must invent forms of political struggle, parties, organisations and movements that work to bring this about.

There are many 'citizens of nowhere' who have populated this book, from the historical figures of the First International, to the unknown migrant, the Amazon workers on strike, or those resisting fascism. Each of these people had a capacity for projecting utopias far into the future and acting in order to realise them, often against all odds. Thanks to such efforts, throughout history we have benefited from social and political progress that all but the most far-sighted citizens of past ages would have regarded as *incredible*. This is the collective capacity we need to recover above all: not expecting or wishing history to come to an end (and certainly not for it to go backwards), but rather being able to move history forwards, which is what politics in its noblest sense should mean for us. This capacity has been taken prisoner at the moment by a global economic system, by an attack on citizenship and on politics itself, which will only be overcome by inventing forms of politics that go beyond the nation state. We have argued that only by inventing a new kind of clock will we set political history in motion again.

Throughout the book we have presented the experience of European Alternatives in attempting to do this over the last ten years, starting from where we are and what we have to work with – which has sometimes seemed very little at first but has turned out to be full of riches and potentials. In writing this book and telling the story, we hope to inspire other citizens of nowhere to roll up their sleeves and join arms with us or start their own transnational initiatives, without thinking that they need anyone's authorisation or support. These things are ours to do.

A Rallying Cry

Ours is not an epoch of rest, and it is not an epoch for looking backwards. It is an epoch of historic change of global proportions. It is up to us to ensure that change is towards political citizenship and collective agency, and not subservience and isolation.

Afterword by
Yanis Varoufakis

Humanity has been globalizing ever since our ancestors left Africa to colonize the planet. A second, powerful wave of globalization came with capitalism whose 'heavy artillery', in Marx and Engels' words, were the 'cheap prices of commodities' that battered 'down all Chinese walls', 'constantly expanding market for its products' and replacing 'the old local and national seclusion and self-sufficiency' with 'intercourse in every direction, universal interdependence of nations'. More recently, in the 1990s, momentous forces were unleashed with the emancipation of capital from all fetters and the inclusion into capitalism's labour markets of an additional two billion people. This type of heavily financialized global capitalism went into a major spasm in 2008 and is now in crisis and, indeed, in retreat.

Looking at the world from an Archimedean distance, financialized globalization has been caught in a steel trap of its making. Its crisis is due to too much money in the wrong hands. Humanity's accumulated savings per capita are at the highest level in history while levels of investment (especially in the things humanity needs, such as green energy) are pitifully low. In the United States, massive sums are accumulating in the accounts of companies and people with no use for them, while those without prospects or good jobs are immersed in mountains of debt. In China, savings approaching half of all income sit side by side with the largest credit bubble imaginable. Europe is even worse: there are countries with gigantic trade surpluses but nowhere to invest them domestically (e.g. Germany and the Netherlands), countries with deficits and no capacity to invest in badly needed labour and capital (e.g. Italy, Spain, Greece) and a eurozone unable to mediate between the two types of countries because it lacks the federal-like institutions that could do this.

And if this never-ending crisis, which was triggered in 2008 and continues today, were not enough, the next crisis is already on the horizon: the rise of the machines. By 2020, almost half the professions in Europe and North America will be susceptible to automation. Robots require a few highly paid designers and operators but may replace millions. This generates labour shortages and labour gluts in the same city, at the same time. The middle class is in for another hollowing out, wage inequality is about to rise again in the richer countries, while developing countries will soon realize that having large young populations offers no respite from poverty. With robots getting smarter and cheaper, de-globalization takes over, and countries such as Nigeria, the Philippines and South Africa will bear the brunt of re-localization (especially with the evolution of 3D printing).

Is it any wonder that globalization's secular crisis begets parochialism, nativism and xenophobia everywhere? Rather than focusing on the role of Facebook, Russia or some unexplained, new-fangled fear of the 'foreigner', the so-called liberal establishment (which is neither liberal nor particularly well-established, judging by recent electoral results in Europe and the US) should look instead at globalization's rotting foundations and realize that an unsustainable system cannot be sustained.

But if globalization is no longer viable, what's next? The answer offered by the alt-right, the xenophobes and those who invest in militant parochialism is clear: return to the bosom of the nation-state, surround yourselves with electrified fences and cut deals between the newly walled realms on the basis of national interest and relative brute strength. The fact that this nightmare is presented as a dream is yet another failure of globalization: Trump, Le Pen, UKIP, the Lega, the AfD and Golden Dawn are symptoms of Barack Obama's and Europe's establishment failure to live up to the expectations they had cultivated with narratives based on ever-globalizing financialized capitalism.

So, what should we do? My view is that only an ambitious new internationalism can help reinvigorate the spirit of humanism at a planetary scale. Lest we forget, our problems are global. Like climate change, they demand local action but also a level of international co-operation not seen since Bretton Woods. Neither North America nor Europe or China can solve them in isolation or even via trade deals. Nothing short of a new

Bretton Woods system can deal with tax injustice, the dearth of good jobs, wage stagnation, public and personal debt, low investment in things we desperately need, too much spending on things that are bad for us, increasing depravity in a world awash with cash, robots that are marginalizing an increasing section of our workforces, prohibitively expensive education that the many need to compete with the robots, etc. National solutions, to be implemented under the deception of 'getting our country back' and behind strengthened border fences, are bound to yield further discontent, as they enable our oligarchs-without-borders to strike trade agreements that condemn the many to a race to the bottom while securing their loot in offshore havens.

Our solutions, therefore, must be global too. But to be so they must undermine at once globalization and parochialism – both the right of capital to move about unimpeded at the expense of waged labour and the fences that stop people and commodities from moving about the planet. In short, our solutions must be internationalist. And the goals of an International New Deal are pressing.

- We need higher wages everywhere, supported by trade agreements and conditions that prevent the Uberization of waged labour domestically.
- Tax havens are crying out for international harmonization, including a simple commitment to deny companies registered in offshore tax havens legal protection of their property rights.

- We desperately need a green energy union focusing on common environmental standards, with the active support of public investment and central banks.
- We should create a New Bretton Woods that recalibrates our financial infrastructure, with one umbrella digital currency in which all trade is denominated in a manner that curtails destabilizing trade surpluses and deficits.
- And we need a universal basic dividend that would be administered by the New Bretton Woods institutions and funded by a percentage of big tech shares deposited in a world wealth fund.

All this sounds utopian. But no more so than the idea that the globalization of the 1990s can be maintained in the twenty-first century or replaced profitably for the majority by a revived nationalism.

Who should pursue this internationalist agenda? Progressives from Europe and North America have a duty to start the ball rolling, courtesy of our collective failure to civilize capitalism. I have no doubt that, if we embark upon this path, others in Asia, Latin America, the Middle East and Africa will soon join us.

As this book argues convincingly, our politics cannot be based on a simple return to nineteenth- or twentieth-century internationalist visions, nor can it be about extending a national conception of politics to a larger, continental, scale (say, the whole of the European Union). Instead, our progressive internationalism must go beyond borders and reimagine political community for the twenty-first century.

At DiEM25, the Democracy in Europe Movement that I proudly co-founded, we take this duty seriously. We are now building Europe's first transnational progressive party, determined to take this internationalist agenda, which we refer to as the European New Deal, to voters across the continent in the May 2019 European Parliament elections. Diem is also present and active in the UK and outside the European Union; indeed, it refuses to be bound by administrative borders. With globalization in retreat and militant parochialism on the rise, we have a moral and political duty to do so.

Notes

Introduction: Citizens of Nowhere

1 See, for example, the Varkey Foundation's Global Citizenship Survey: Emma Broadbent, John Gougoulis, Nicole Lui, Vikas Pota and Jonathan Simons, *Generation Z: Global citizenship survey*, London: Varkey Foundation, 2017, www.varkeyfoundation.org/sites/default/files/Global%20Young%20People%20Report%20%28digital%29%20NEW%20%281%29.pdf. It is interesting to note that for the first time in 2016, after fifteen years of polling, the Globescan global attitudes survey conducted for the BBC World Service found that nearly one in two people see themselves as global citizens rather than as national citizens, and that the increase was driven by people from non-OECD countries including Nigeria (73 per cent), China (71 per cent), Peru (70 per cent) and India (67 per cent); available at www.globescan.com/news-and-analysis/press-releases/press-releases-2016/103-press-releases-2016/383-global-citizenship-a-growing-sentiment-among-citizens-of-emerging-economies-global-poll.html.

2 See, for example, the European Parliament's special Eurobarometer survey of the attitudes of young people in 2016; available at www.europarl.europa.eu/pdf/eurobarometre/2016/eye2016/eb85_1_eye_2016_analytical_overview_en.pdf.

3 In 2014, in the midst of the ongoing Ukraine–Russia war, Angela Merkel famously required her cabinet to read Christopher Clark's historical account of the origins of the First World War *The Sleepwalkers: How Europe went to war in 1914*, London: Penguin, 2013, and to take a day out to discuss it directly with the historian.

4 William Morris, *News from Nowhere and Other Writings*, London: Penguin, 1994.

5 Edward Bellamy, *Looking Backward: 2000–1887*, London: Tickner & Co., 1888.

6 Max Weber, reprinted in Chapter 7 in *Weber's Rationalism and Modern Society*, translated by Tony Waters and Dagmar Waters, New York and Basingstoke: Palgrave Macmillan, 2015.

1 Broken Clocks

1 Amartya Sen, among many others, had been making this point since 2011. See Amartya Sen, 'It isn't just the euro: Europe's democracy itself is at stake', *Guardian*, 22 June 2011, www.theguardian.com/commentisfree/2011/jun/22/euro-europes-democracy-rating-agencies.

2 Peter Spiegel, 'Donald Tusk interview: the annotated transcript', *Financial Times* Brussels blog, 17 July 2015, www.ft.com/content/ff50e5a9-7b15-3998-a9f1-c11359dc01b8.

3 Private conversation with 'Zhang Ying'. The name is a pseudonym.

4 As reported by former *Financial Times* Beijing bureau chief Richard McGregor: 'Could Trump's blundering lead to war between China and Japan?', *Guardian*, 17 August 2017, www.theguardian.com/world/2017/aug/17/could-trumps-blundering-lead-to-war-between-china-and-japan.

5 One recalls the 1989 Tiananmen repression and the acceleration of the capitalist transformation of China as outcomes.

6 On the other hand, as Antonio Gramsci was to note in the early twentieth century, we also discovered that there is no one-to-one match between the immediate material interests of individuals and their political expressions in parliamentary elections. Rather, the elites maintain the capacity to shift the terms of the debate and of common sense, often against the material interests of the popular classes, by exercising their social, cultural and discursive hegemony. A classic example is the majority support from women for patriarchal, Catholic parties.

7 2018 marks the hundredth anniversary of the Representation of the People Act in the United Kingdom, which gave the vote to propertied women over the age of thirty and all men over the age of twenty-one. It also marks 100 years since individuals could join the Labour Party, which previously was a coalition of socialist, labour and progressive organisations.

8 The quote is from one of Zola's masterpieces, *Germinal*, which tells the story of a coalminers' strike in northern France in the 1860s.

9 David Graeber, *Bullshit Jobs: A theory*, New York: Simon & Schuster, 2018.

10 The numbers are staggering: Uber stands accused of having subtracted up to US$800 million from the labour share it should have paid on its services through the use of contractual forms reversing the social protections normally covered by the employer. See Dan Levine and Heather Somerville, 'Uber drivers, if employees, owed $730 million more: US court papers', Reuters, 9 May 2016, www.reuters.com/article/us-uber-tech-drivers-lawsuit/uber-drivers-if-employees-owed-730-million-more-u-s-court-papers-idUSKCN0Y02E8.

11 Many reports have been written about the inequalities of the German labour market, notably following the draconian welfare reforms known as Hartz IV. For a good-quality overview, see Olivier Cyran, 'Germany's working poor', *The Nation*, 6 September 2017, www.thenation.com/article/germanys-working-poor/. For a comparative analysis of in-work poverty in EU countries, see Eurofound, *In-work Poverty in the EU*, Luxembourg: Publications Office of the European Union, 2017, www.eurofound.europa.eu/sites/default/files/ef_publication/field_ef_document/ef1725en.pdf. This report puts Germany second only to Romania for the risk of in-work poverty.

12 See UNICEF, 'Building the future: children and the sustainable development goals in rich countries', Innocenti Report Card 14, Florence: UNICEF, 2017, www.unicef.org/media/media_96452.html.

13 See Andrew Hood and Tom Waters, 'Living standards, poverty, and inequality in the UK', London: Institute for Fiscal Studies, www.ifs.org.uk/publications/10028.

14 Data elaborated in September 2017 by the Research Institute of the Italian Industrial Confederation.

15 See Branka Trivić, 'Michael Kirby Srbiji: Izvozite robu, a ne mlade ljude' (report from the Kopaonik Business Forum), Radio Slobonda Evropa, 5 March 2015, www.slobodnaevropa.org/a/ michael-kirby-srbiji-izvozite-robu-a-ne-mlade-ljude/26883811. html.

16 Michael Hirsh, 'Can Obama Save Capitalism?', *Newsweek*, 12 November 2008, www.newsweek.com/hirsh-can-obama-save-capitalism-84683.

17 See Editorial, 'Obama's TARP team helped banks, betrayed homeowners', *Washington Examiner*, 23 July 2012, www. washingtonexaminer.com/examiner-editorial-obamas-tarp-team-helped-banks-betrayed-homeowners/article/2502917.

18 Naomi Klein, *No Is Not Enough*, Chicago: Haymarket Books, 2017.

19 In 2016, Harvard University polled young adults between the ages of eighteen and twenty-nine and found that 51 per cent did not support capitalism, while 42 per cent claimed they did.

20 CNN 'Town Hall' meeting with Nancy Pelosi, 31 January 2017.

21 We use here a phrase employed by Étienne Balibar to describe the European response to the Eurocrisis, which itself recalls the strategy of conservatives in Spain at the turn of the twentieth century to reorganise and consolidate the country in a post-disaster context, fearful of a 'revolution from below' if they did nothing.

22 Peter Muller, René Pfister and Christoph Schult, 'Chancellor Merkel's dangerous lack of passion for Europe', Spiegel Online, 18 July 2011, www.spiegel.de/international/europe/ rudderless-eu-chancellor-merkel-s-dangerous-lack-of-passion-for-europe-a-775085.html.

23 Since the passing of the Lisbon Treaty in 2007, it is possible for 1 million European citizens signing a petition to call for the European Commission to take the initiative on an issue falling under European competence. Ours was one of the first European Citizens Initiative (ECIs) registered, and our main objective was to get the European Commission to acknowledge that they have some responsibility regarding media pluralism issues (they had often denied this). We collected over 200,000 signatures. Since 2017, the ECI legislation has been under review by the Commission to improve its functioning.

24 See https://citizenspact.eu/.

25 Christine Wang, 'Michael Moore says Trump is a "human Molotov cocktail" supporters get to throw', CNBC, 4 November 2016, www.cnbc.com/2016/11/04/michael-moore-says-trump-is-a-human-molotov-cocktail-supporters-get-to-throw.html.

26 See Beppe Grillo, 'Il vaffanculo di Trump', Il Blog delle Stelle, 9 November 2016, www.ilblogdellestelle.it/il_vaffanculo_dil_vaffanculo_di_trump.html.

27 Hannah Arendt wrote about the perverse loneliness of totalitarian systems, in which everyone is suspicious of others and terrorised by the state. A similar set of symptoms are shown in our contemporary Western authoritarian regimes. For an artistic portrayal of this, see, for example, the film *White God* by contemporary Hungarian director Kornél Mundruczó.

28 Antonio Gramsci, *Selections from the Prison Notebooks*, translated by Q. Hoarse and G. Nowell Smith, New York: International Publishers, 1971, pp. 275–6.

29 W. B. Yeats, 'The Second Coming' in *Collected Poems*, London: Picador, 1990, p. 211.

30 See Edmund S. Higgins, 'Is mental health declining in the US?', *Scientific American*, 1 January 2017, www.scientificamerican.com/article/is-mental-health-declining-in-the-u-s/.

31 See European College of Neuropsychopharmacology, 'The size and burden of mental disorders in Europe', *Science Daily*, 6 September 2011, www.sciencedaily.com/releases/2011/09/110905074609.htm.

32 European Commission, *EU Youth Report 2015*, Luxembourg: Publications Office of the European Union, 2016, ec.europa.eu/assets/eac/youth/library/reports/youth-report-2015_en.pdf, p. 239ff.

33 There are many ways for political institutions to wither away. A supranational construction such as the European Union, lacking a clear and legitimate method for 'changing the government' of the EU, is at particular risk of outright disintegration. National democracies may enter an existential crisis through new independentist claims, by sending extreme parties or leaders to power, or, simply, by driving a permanent wedge between the representatives and the represented.

34 Herbert A. Simon, *Sciences of the Artificial*, Boston: MIT Press, 1996, 5ff.

2 The Wizard of Oz

1 Karl Polanyi, *The Great Transformation*, Boston MA: Beacon Press, 2001, p. 145.

2 F. A. Hayek, 'The principles of liberal social order', *Il Politico* 31 (4), December 1966: 601–18.

3 Ordoliberalism, or the German variant of neoliberalism, theorises fully the new role for the state. A market order (*ordo*) does not emerge spontaneously, but rather requires constant public activism to maintain a regulatory framework capable of guaranteeing market freedoms. The market is freed by the discipline imposed on everything else. In the words of Walter Eucken, one of the founders of ordoliberal thinking, what is needed is nothing short of an 'economic constitution': one capable of guaranteeing the prerogatives of rights of capital and the duty of the state. And so the state – and this is the point – far from being emptied out emerges transformed and placed at the service of the market. In addition, the state acts constantly to define and police what counts as valuable in society, and to open up this realm to ever greater economic competition and consumerism. All this requires a political class that is willing, like the dwarf in our story, to hide in the machine in order to guarantee its functioning.

Notes

4 Robert Owen, *Observations on the Effect of the Manufacturing System: With hints for the improvement of those parts of it which are most injurious to health and morals*, London, Edinburgh and Glasgow: Longman, Hurst, Rees, Orme and Brown, 1817. Available online at www.marxists.org/reference/subject/economics/owen/observations.htm.

5 Gunther Teubner, following in the footsteps of Niklas Luhmann, has led pioneering work on this process of what he calls 'constitutional fragmentation'. See in particular, Gunther Teubner, *Constitutional Fragments*, Oxford: Oxford University Press, 2012. See also Catherine Colliot-Thélène, *La Démocratie sans Demos*, Paris: Presses Universitaires de France, 2011.

6 See, for instance, John Darwin, *After Tamerlane: The rise and fall of global empires, 1400–2000*, London: Penguin, 2008.

7 Jeffry A. Frieden, *Global Capitalism: Its fall and rise in the 20th century*, New York: W. W. Norton & Company, 2007.

8 Jacob Viner, 'Conflicts of principle in drafting a trade charter' (report from the GATT negotiations), *Foreign Affairs*, 25 January 1947, p. 613.

9 Keynes famously proposed a Bank of International Settlements and a supranational currency, the Bancor. His internationalist view was overtaken by that of American economist Harry Dexter White, who imposed an international system rotating instead around the primacy of the US dollar as the world's reserve currency.

10 Nancy Fraser, 'A triple movement?', *New Left Review* 81, May–June 2013.

11 'Brussels rattled as China reaches out to Eastern Europe', *Financial Times*, 28 November 2017.

12 For a readable analysis of how China's contemporary attitude to globalisation is guided by its history, see Howard French, *Everything Under the Heavens: How the past helps shape China's push for global power*, New York: Knopf, 2017.

13 Philippe Van Parijs drew attention to the importance of this text

in his Max Weber lecture at the European University Institute in November 2016.

14 'The economic conditions of interstate federalism', originally printed in *New Commonwealth Quarterly* V (2), September 1939: 131–49, here quoted from F. A. Hayek, *Individualism and Economic Order*, Chicago: University of Chicago Press, 1948, pp. 255–72.

15 Ibid: 258.

16 Ibid: 261.

17 Ibid: 262.

18 Ibid: 265.

19 Prizes offered to some corporate investors are increasingly resembling capitulation to any and every demand, even in relatively wealthy parts of the world. For example, when Amazon called for bids from cities to host its new 'second headquarters' in the USA of up to 50,000 employees, it received over 230 offers. Chicago offered to allow Amazon to keep US$1.32 billion of income taxes paid by its own workers (i.e. the workers paying the bosses their taxes). Boston offered an 'Amazon task force' of city employees to work on behalf of the company. Fresno, California, offered that Amazon jointly decide with the city administration how the company's taxes should be spent. As Danny Westneat has suggested in revealing this information in *The Seattle Times*, 'Now a single company is viewed as so valuable that some seem ready to wave the flag on the whole "for the people, by the people" experiment.' See Danny Westneat, 'This City Hall, brought to you by Amazon', *The Seattle Times*, 24 November 2017.

20 William Morris, 'Review of Bellamy's *Looking Backward*', *Commonweal*, 21 June 1889.

21 The emergence of 'nation branding' as an industry in recent years along with an apparently endless appetite among the readership of certain magazines and internet sites for league tables of 'the best city to live in', 'the best country to be born in' or 'the best passport to have' are symptoms of this. For more on the commodification of citizenship in particular, see Chapter 3.

22 'What you are running here is not a factory, it is a zoo. But in a zoo there are many types of animals. Some are monkeys who dance on your fingertips, others are lions who can bite your head off. We are the lions, Mr Manager' (Jayaben Desai, leader of the Grunwick picket, 1976–78).

23 For an analysis of and interviews with delivery workers organising across borders, see Lorenzo Zamponi, 'Workers of all apps, unite!' in *A Guide to Transnational Activism*, Siegen, Germany: TransSOL, 2018.

24 Callum Cant, 'Precarious couriers are leading the struggle against platform capitalism', *Political Critique*, 3 August 2017, http://politicalcritique.org/world/2017/precarious-couriers-are-leading-the-struggle-against-platform-capitalism/.

25 For more information, see the Transnational Social Strike website at www.transnational-strike.info, which has details of cross-border meetings and coordination between workers.

26 Ralf Rukus, 'Confronting Amazon', *Jacobin*, 31 March 2016, www.jacobinmag.com/2016/03/amazon-poland-poznan-strikes-workers.

27 It should be noted that this legislation is currently being reviewed and revised by the European authorities.

28 See the exchange project 'Transnational Dialogue', which engaged Europe, China and Brazil in a multi-year cultural and political exchange that we fostered between 2011 and 2016 (www.transnationaldialogues.eu).

29 'Mini-jobs' is a term coined in Germany to characterise part-time work, exempt from income tax, where the salary is lower than €450 per month. The system of these mini-job contracts was developed by the German government to allow employers to pay less social security insurance. The scheme is widely criticised for artificially reducing unemployment statistics, creating in-work poverty, undermining employment contracts and depressing pay.

30 Yanis Varoufakis, *Adults in the Room: My battle with Europe's deep establishment*, New York: Random House, 2017.

31 Edmund Burke, speech to the electors of Bristol, 1774.

32 Jean Monnet, speech to the National Press Club, Washington DC, 30 April 1952.

33 A recent study by the Centre for Economics and Business Research found that ordinary booksellers pay eleven times more tax than Amazon. See Alison Flood, 'Amazon "pays 11 times less corporation tax than traditional booksellers"', *Guardian*, 12 September 2017, https://amp.theguardian.com/books/2017/sep/12/amazon-pays-11-times-less-corporation-tax-than-traditional-booksellers.

34 The Netherlands, Ireland, Luxembourg and Cyprus are among the world's fifteen worst corporate tax havens according to research by Oxfam International. The United Kingdom does not feature on the list, but four territories that the United Kingdom is ultimately responsible for do appear: the Cayman Islands, Jersey, Bermuda and the British Virgin Islands. Reports on the matter abound: see, for instance, 'Tax battles: the dangerous race to the bottom on corporate tax', Oxfam policy paper, 12 December 2016, www.oxfam.org/en/research/tax-battles-dangerous-global-race-bottom-corporate-tax. For a compelling overview, see Nicholas Shaxson, *Treasure Islands: Tax havens and the men who stole the world*, London: Bodley Head, 2010.

35 See Marc Auerbach, *Ikea: Flat pack tax avoidance*, a study commissioned by the Greens/EFA Group in the European Parliament, 2016, www.greens-efa.eu/en/article/corporate-tax-avoidance-5963/.

36 See Jeppe Kofod and Michael Theurer, 'Report on tax rulings and other measures similar in nature or effect (2016/2038(INI))', Brussels: European Parliament, 2016, www.europarl.europa.eu/sides/getDoc.do?pubRef=-//EP//NONSGML+REPORT+A8-2016-0223+0+DOC+PDF+V0//EN.

37 The work of whistle-blowers has recently made this practice very evident; among them, the Luxembourg Leaks scandal highlighting the web of corporate favours woven by the small

European state. It is a pity that the people responsible for the leak have been brought to court, whereas the man responsible for crafting the Luxembourg structure of tax dodging was elected president of the European Commission in 2014.

38 This is more than a sectoral delay; rather, this is an entire *industry* that Europe lacks almost entirely. It would only be moderate hyperbole to state that Europe's position is not too distant from that of nineteenth-century India when steam power – which had the equivalent impact of the internet at the time – first made its appearance. This process locked in the rest of the world's dependency on European industrial powerhouses, producing the early de-industrialisation of the global periphery and propelling European states to global economic and political dominance. See Stephen D. King, *Grave New World: The end of globalization, the return of history*, New Haven: Yale University Press, 2017, p. 176.

39 Evgeny Morozov, 'Data populists must seize our information – for the benefit of all', *Guardian*, 4 December 2016, www.theguardian.com/commentisfree/2016/dec/04/data-populists-must-seize-information-for-benefit-of-all-evgeny-morozov.

40 The review of the European Union's Generalised System of Preferences (GSP), currently under way, provides an opportunity for reform in this sense. The GSP is a preferential system of tariffs that allows for exemption from World Trade Organization (WTO) rules relating to the most favoured nation principle, which obliges WTO members to offer to all other members the same terms as they offer to any favoured member. GSP allows WTO members to lower tariffs for the least economically developed countries. Since 2014, the European Union, by developing a GSP+ status, has required less economically developed countries that want to benefit from lower tariffs for entry to the single market to ratify and respect UN and International Labour Organisation conventions, providing a basis for discussion of human rights, civic space and labour rights issues with the countries; civil society in those countries has been effective

in using this process. At the moment, this practice is not well established, with a lack of guidelines, procedures, incentives and sanctions, but it could develop into a powerful space for civil society to promote human rights. NGOs such as ACT Alliance EU, the Clean Clothes Campaign, the International Federation for Human Rights and the International Trade Union Confederation have been developing a GSP reform platform for this purpose.

3 If Europe Is a Fortress We Are All in Prison

1 Hannah Arendt, 'We refugees', *Menorah Journal*, 1 January 1943.

2 See https://best-hotel-in-europe.eu.

3 Eleonora Camilli, 'One year at City Plaza in Athens', *Political Critique*, 28 June 2017, http://politicalcritique.org/world/eu/2017/camilli-city-plaza-athens-refugees/.

4 See the full proposals on the website of the initiative as www.lacartadilampedusa.org.

5 Migreurop identified capacity of at least 47,000 in the camps (see www.migreurop.org/article2747.html?lang=fr), whereas the Global Detention Project (www.globaldetentionproject.org) has identified much higher figures.

6 This is according to Migreurop (see www.migreurop.org/article2488.html?lang=fr).

7 See Jessica Elgot, 'Number of EU citizens detained in UK up by 27%, figures show', *Guardian*, 23 August 2017, www.theguardian.com/uk-news/2017/aug/23/number-of-eu-citizens-detained-in-uk-up-by-27-figures-show.

8 According to the Association of Visitors to Immigration Detainees, for example, in 2016 in the UK, 28,661 people left detention: 47 per cent were removed from the UK and 53 per cent of those detained were released back into the community. In 2016, the longest recorded length of detention was 1,333 days: over three and a half years. In 2017, the Italian Senate found that, in the first nine months of 2016, only 44 per cent of people detained were deported, and in 2015 the percentage

was around 50 per cent. Despite this limited 'effectiveness', the Italian government is planning on a significant increase in detention. See Commissione Straordinaria per la Tutela e la Promozione dei Diritti Umani, 'Rapporto sui Centri di Identificazione ed Espulsione in Italia', Rome: Senate of the Republic, 2017, www.senato.it/application/xmanager/projects/leg17/file/repository/commissioni/dirittiumaniXVII/allegati/Cie_rapporto_aggiornato_2_gennaio_2017.pdf. It is even doubtful whether detention centres contribute to a 'hostile environment', if that means that they play any significant role in deterring migration. The Global Roundtable on Alternatives to Detention of Asylum-Seekers, Migrants and Stateless Persons of the UN High Commissioner for Refugees (UNHCR) found in July 2011 that: 'There is no empirical evidence that detention deters migration, or discourages people from seeking asylum' (see the summary conclusions of the Roundtable at www.unhcr.org/uk/protection/expert/536a00576/global-roundtable-alternatives-detention-asylum-seekers-refugees-migrants.html). The 'hostile environment' is mostly for show to domestic audiences.

9 See closethecamps.org and Mary Bosworth, 'The impact of immigration detention on mental health: a literature review' in Stephen Shaw, *Review into the Welfare in Detention of Vulnerable Persons: A report to the Home Office*, Cm 9186, London: HMSO, 2016, www.gov.uk/government/uploads/system/uploads/attachment_data/file/490782/52532_Shaw_Review_Accessible.pdf.

10 For more on this theme, see Étienne Balibar, *Equaliberty*, translated by James Ingham, Durham NC: Duke University Press, 2014.

11 The inscription on the statue of Thomas Paine in the Parc Montsouris in Paris reads: 'Intellectual, pamphleteer and revolutionary, Thomas Paine, Citizen of the World (1737–1809). English by birth, French by decree, and American by adoption.'

12 See Patrick Weil, *Qu'est-ce qu'un français?*, Paris: Grasset, 2002.

13 When Theresa May was Home Secretary, she usually stripped away British citizenship when people were out of the country, leaving them with no practical way of appealing, or even knowing why they had lost their citizenship. This is May's early vision of citizens of nowhere, before it is repackaged and generalised by the Brexit referendum. At least two British people who lost their citizenship in this way were subsequently killed in US drone strikes: a phenomenon that may make us realise that denationalisation can be a form of death penalty, but with even less judicial process.

14 Supreme Court Justice Hugo Black said in 1967, in a judgment that made it impossible for the US to remove citizenship: 'In our country, the people are sovereign and the Government cannot sever its relationship to the people by taking away their citizenship.' This judgment shows the struggle between popular sovereignty and state sovereignty when it comes to citizenship, and decides in favour of popular sovereignty. See Patrick Weil, 'Can a citizen be sovereign?', *Humanity Journal* blog, 2 January 2016, http://humanityjournal.org/blog/can-a-citizen-be-sovereign/.

15 See Balakrishnan Prabhu, '35+ best countries for buying citizenship or residency', *Corpocrat Magazine*, 22 December 2016, https://corpocrat.com/2016/12/22/30-countries-for-buying-citizenship-through-investment/.

16 See Sara Farolfi, David Pegg and Stelios Orphanides, 'Cyprus "selling" EU citizenship to super rich of Russia and Ukraine', *Guardian*, 17 September 2017, www.theguardian.com/world/2017/sep/17/cyprus-selling-eu-citizenship-to-super-rich-of-russia-and-ukraine.

17 See Joe Myers, 'Countries where you can buy citizenship', World Economic Forum, 28 July 2016, www.weforum.org/agenda/2016/07/countries-selling-citizenship/.

18 See Kim Gittleson, 'Where is the cheapest place to buy citizenship?', BBC News, 4 June 2014, www.bbc.com/news/business-27674135.

19 See 'Slovak PM: We can't integrate "our own" Roma, to say nothing of refugees', Romea.cz, 2 September 2015, www.romea.cz/en/news/world/slovak-pm-we-can-t-integrate-our-own-roma-to-say-nothing-of-refugees.

20 'We cannot take the misery of the whole world' is a phrase of the French socialist Michel Rocard from 1989, which has since been ceaselessly used by the far right against migration, to suggest that France already has its share of the misery, and the misery of the whole world would simply overwhelm it (as if the whole world would move to France alone on the planet). Of course, aside from being absurd, the phrase overlooks the fact that migrants do not bring only misery … We could multiply indefinitely examples of this kind of ethnocentric racist demagogy.

21 Michel Foucault, 'Face aux gouvernements, les droits de l'homme', *Liberation* 967, 30 June–1 July 1984, p. 22. Published in *Dits et écrits (1954–1988). Vol. IV: 1980–1988*, Paris: Éditions Gallimard, 1994, pp. 707–8 (355).

4 Beyond Internationalism: A Transnational Interdependence Party

1 Michel Foucault, 'Face aux gouvernements, les droits de l'homme', *Liberation* 967, 30 June–1 July 1984, p. 22. Published in *Dits et écrits (1954–1988). Vol. IV: 1980–1988*, Paris: Éditions Gallimard, 1994, pp. 707–8 (355).

2 In *An Introduction to the Principles of Morals and Legislation*, London: Printed for T. Payne and Son, 1789. Interestingly, Bentham limits the usage to the relationship between the sovereign representatives of the states, and says that the relationships between private individuals belonging to different states would be covered by internal law.

3 Giuseppe Mazzini, 'Towards a holy alliance of the peoples' (1849) in *A Cosmopolitanism of Nations*, translated by Stefano Recchia and edited by Stefano Recchia and Nadia Urbinati, Princeton: Princeton University Press, 2009, p. 126.

4 Marcel Mauss, 'La nation et l'internationalisme' in *Cohésion*

sociale et division de la sociologie. Oeuvres III, Paris: Éditions de Minuit, 1969, pp. 626–34. The full draft text of 'The nation' has been gathered and published in French in Marcel Fournier and Jean Terrier (eds), *La nation: Éléments de politique modern*, Paris: Presses Universitaires de France, 2013.

5 Mikhail Bakunin, *Revolutionary Catechism*, 1851. Available online at www.marxists.org/reference/archive/bakunin/works/1866/catechism.htm.

6 In the *German Ideology*, Marx and Engels write: 'Empirically communism is only possible as the act of the ruling peoples, "at one stroke" and simultaneously, which presupposes the universal development of the productive force and the global economy which goes along with that.'

7 Karl Kautsky, *The Class Struggle (Erfurt Program)*, 1888.

8 Ursula Hirschmann, *Noi Senza Patria*, Bologna: Il Mulino, 1993. Here quoted in our translation from the French translation *Nous Sans Patrie*, translated by M. Gaille, Paris: Les Belles Lettres, 2009.

9 Ibid., p. 121.

10 Ibid., p. 20.

11 The title of Ursula Hirschmann's biography makes reference to the famous quote of Nietzsche in *The Gay Science*:

> We who are homeless are too diverse and racially mixed in our descent, as 'modern men', and consequently we are not inclined to participate in the mendacious racial self-admiration and obscenity that parades in Germany today as a sign of a German way of thinking and this is doubly false and indecent amongst the people of the 'historical sense'. In a word – and let this be our word of honour – we are good Europeans, the rich heirs of millennia of European spirit, with too many provisions but also too many obligations.
>
> *The Gay Science*, translated by J. Nauckhoff and edited by B. Williams, Cambridge: Cambridge University Press, 2001, p. 242

Notes

12 For a full analysis of the World Social Forum, its achievements and its shortfalls, see Boaventura de Sousa Santos, *The Rise of the Global Left: The World Social Forum and beyond*, Chicago: Chicago University Press, 2006.

13 John Holloway, *Changing the World without Taking Power*, London: Pluto Press, 2002.

14 Tom Mitchell, 'China softens tone in drive for Asia influence', *Financial Times*, 4 January 2017, www.ft.com/content/4e96e20c-e742-11e7-97e2-916d4fbac0da.

15 In a way, the party would take the 'view from nowhere', but not in the sense of having the pretence of a scientific, objective, abstract or detached view from above; rather, in the sense of taking a highly situated point of view, but one that is currently supposed not to exist. In *The View from Nowhere*, Thomas Nagel contrasts the objective point of view from subjective points of views in ethics and science, but does not touch on politics. See Thomas Nagel, *The View from Nowhere*, Oxford: Oxford University Press, 1996. For a critique of the kind of Enlightenment cosmopolitanism we do not advocate, see also Stephen Toulmin, *Cosmopolis: the hidden agenda of modernity*, Chicago: University of Chicago Press, 1990.

16 A recent mathematical modelling applied to social study seeks to demonstrate that the likelihood of higher-level cooperation, such as that required to tackle global challenges including climate change, increases as local bonds and cooperation increase at the closest level, such as that of the neighbourhood. See Benjamin Allen, 'Evolutionary dynamics on any population structure', *Nature* 544, April 2017: 227–30.

17 For a far-sighted reconceptualisation of the relationship between domestic and foreign in the context of globalisation, see the seminal text of R. B. J. Walker, *Inside/Outside: International relations as political theory*, Cambridge: Cambridge University Press, 1992.

18 For a historically rich and sociologically alert overview of the February 2017 anti-corruption protests in Romania, see Ovidiu

Tichindeleanu, 'Romania's protests: from social justice to class politics', *CriticAtac*, 27 February 2017, www.criticatac.ro/romanias-protests-from-social-justice-to-class-politics/.

19 Benjamin Barber, *If Mayors Ruled the World*, New Haven: Yale University Press, 2013.

20 For a good overview rich in references for further reading, see Beppe Caccia, 'From citizen platforms to fearless cities: Europe's new municipalism', *Political Critique*, June 2017, http://politicalcritique.org/world/2017/from-citizen-platforms-to-fearless-cities-europes-new-municipalism/.

21 Titus Livius, *The History of Rome: Book 2*, Cambridge MA: Harvard University Press, 1919, Chapter 32.

22 TTIP is the proposed Transatlantic Trade and Investment Partnership between the EU and the US, and CETA is the Comprehensive Economic and Trade Agreement between Canada and the EU.

Bibliography and Further Reading

Auerbach, Marc. *Ikea: Flat pack tax avoidance*. Study commissioned by the Greens/EFA Group in the European Parliament, 2016, www.greens-efa.eu/en/article/corporate-tax-avoidance-5963/.

Bakunin, Mikhail. *Revolutionary Catechism*, 1851, www.marxists.org/reference/archive/bakunin/works/1866/catechism.htm.

Balibar, Étienne. *Equaliberty*. Translated by James Ingham. Durham NC: Duke University Press, 2014.

Balibar, Étienne. *Europe: Crise et fin?* Paris: Éditions Le Bord de l'Eau, 2016.

Barber, Benjamin. *If Mayors Ruled the World*. New Haven: Yale University Press, 2013.

Bellamy, Edward. *Looking Backward: 2000–1887*. London: Tickner & Co., 1888.

Bentham, Jeremy. *An Introduction to the Principles of Morals and Legislation*. London: Printed for T. Payne and Son, 1789.

Bosworth, Mary. 'The impact of immigration detention on mental health: a literature review' in Stephen Shaw, *Review into the Welfare in Detention of Vulnerable Persons: A report to the Home Office*. Cm 9186. London: HMSO, 2016, www.gov.uk/government/uploads/system/uploads/attachment_data/file/490782/52532_Shaw_Review_Accessible.pdf.

Broadbent, Emma, John Gougoulis, Nicole Lui, Vikas Pota and Jonathan Simons. *Generation Z: Global citizenship survey*. London: Varkey Foundation, 2017, www.varkeyfoundation.org/sites/default/files/Global%20Young%20People%20 Report%20%28digital%29%20NEW%20%281%29.pdf.

Clark, Christopher. *The Sleepwalkers: How Europe went to war in 1914*. London: Penguin, 2013.

Colliot-Thélène, Catherine. *La Démocratie sans Demos*. Paris: Presses Universitaires de France, 2011.

Commissione Straordinaria per la Tutela e la Promozione dei Diritti Umani. 'Rapporto sui Centri di Identificazione ed Espulsione in Italia'. Rome: Senate of the Republic, 2017, www. senato.it/application/xmanager/projects/leg17/file/repository/ commissioni/dirittiumaniXVII/allegati/Cie_rapporto_aggiornato_2_gennaio_2017.pdf.

Darwin, John. *After Tamerlane: The rise and fall of global empires, 1400–2000*. London: Penguin, 2008.

Delmas-Marty, Mireille. *Aux Quatres Vents du Monde*. Paris: Éditions du Seuil, 2016.

de Sousa Santos, Boaventura. *The Rise of the Global Left: The World Social Forum and beyond*. Chicago: Chicago University Press, 2006.

Eribon, Didier. *Retour à Reims*. Paris: Éditions Flammarion, 2010.

Eurofound. *In-work Poverty in the EU*. Luxembourg: Publications Office of the European Union, 2017, www.eurofound.europa. eu/sites/default/files/ef_publication/field_ef_document/ ef1725en.pdf.

European Commission. *EU Youth Report 2015*. Luxembourg: Publications Office of the European Union, 2016, ec.europa.eu/ assets/eac/youth/library/reports/youth-report-2015_en.pdf.

Foucault, Michel. *Dits et écrits (1954–1988). Vol. IV: 1980–1988*. Paris: Éditions Gallimard, 1994.

Fournier, Marcel and Jean Terrier (eds), *La nation: Éléments de politique modern*. Paris: Presses Universitaires de France, 2013.

French, Howard. *Everything Under the Heavens: How the past helps shape China's push for global power*. New York: Knopf, 2017.

Frieden, Jeffry A. *Global Capitalism: Its fall and rise in the 20th century*. New York: W. W. Norton & Company, 2007.

Bibliography

Graeber, David. *Bullshit Jobs: A theory*. New York: Simon & Schuster, 2018.

Gramsci, Antonio. *Selections from the Prison Notebooks*. Translated by Q. Hoarse and G. Nowell Smith. New York: International Publishers, 1971.

Hardt, Michael and Antonio Negri. *Assembly*. Oxford: Oxford University Press, 2017.

Hayek, F. A. *Individualism and Economic Order*. Chicago: University of Chicago Press, 1948.

Hirschmann, Ursula. *Noi Senza Patria*. Bologna: Il Mulino, 1993. In French: *Nous Sans Patrie*. Translated by M. Gaille. Paris: Les Belles Lettres, 2009.

Holloway, John. *Changing the World without Taking Power*. London: Pluto Press, 2002.

Hood, Andrew and Tom Waters. 'Living standards, poverty, and inequality in the UK'. London: Institute for Fiscal Studies, www.ifs.org.uk/publications/10028.

Judis, John. *The Populist Explosion: How the great recession transformed American and European politics*. New York: Columbia Global Reports, 2016.

Kautsky, Karl. *The Class Struggle (Erfurt Program)*, 1888.

King, Stephen D. *Grave New World: The end of globalization, the return of history*. New Haven: Yale University Press, 2017.

Klein, Naomi. *No Is Not Enough*. Chicago: Haymarket Books, 2017.

Kofod, Jeppe and Michael Theurer. 'Report on tax rulings and other measures similar in nature or effect (2016/2038(INI))'. Brussels: European Parliament, 2016, www.europarl.europa.eu/sides/getDoc.do?pubRef=-//EP//NONSGML+REPORT+A8-2016-0223+0+DOC+PDF+V0//EN.

Luce, Edward. *The Retreat of Western Liberalism*. London: Little, Brown, 2017.

Mahbubani, Kishore. *The Great Convergence: Asia, the West, and the logic of one world*. New York: PublicAffairs, 2014.

Marx, Karl and Friedrich Engels. *The German Ideology*. Moscow: Progress Publishers.

Mauss, Marcel. *Cohésion sociale et division de la sociologie. Oeuvres III*. Paris: Éditions de Minuit, 1969.

Mazover, Mark. *Governing the World: The history of an idea*. New York: Penguin, 2013.

Mazzini, Giuseppe. *A Cosmopolitanism of Nations*. Translated by Stefano Recchia and edited by Stefano Recchia and Nadia Urbinati. Princeton: Princeton University Press, 2009.

Morris, William. *News from Nowhere and Other Writings*. London: Penguin, 1994.

Nagel, Thomas. *The View from Nowhere*. Oxford: Oxford University Press, 1996.

Nietzsche, Friedrich. *The Gay Science*. Translated by J. Nauckhoff and edited by B. Williams. Cambridge: Cambridge University Press, 2001.

Owen, Robert. *Observations on the Effect of the Manufacturing System: With hints for the improvement of those parts of it which are most injurious to health and morals*. London, Edinburgh and Glasgow: Longman, Hurst, Rees, Orme and Brown, 1817, www.marxists.org/reference/subject/economics/owen/observations.htm.

Polanyi, Karl. *The Great Transformation*. Boston MA: Beacon Press, 2001.

Shaxson, Nicholas. *Treasure Islands: Tax havens and the men who stole the world*. London: Bodley Head, 2010.

Simon, Herbert A. *Sciences of the Artificial*. Boston: MIT Press, 1996.

Spinelli, Barbara. *La sovranità assente*. Torino: Einaudi Editore, 2014.

Srnicek, Nick. *Platform Capitalism*. London: Polity Press, 2016.

Subirats, Joan. *El poder de lo proximo*. Barcelona: Los Libros de la Catarata, 2016.

Teubner, Gunther. *Constitutional Fragments*. Oxford: Oxford University Press, 2012.

Titus Livius (Livy). *The History of Rome*. Cambridge MA: Harvard University Press, 1919.

Toulmin, Stephen. *Cosmopolis: the hidden agenda of modernity*. Chicago: University of Chicago Press, 1990.

Bibliography

TransSOL. *A Guide to Transnational Activism*, Siegen, Germany: TransSOL, 2018.

UNICEF. 'Building the future: children and the sustainable development goals in rich countries'. Innocenti Report Card 14. Florence: UNICEF, 2017, www.unicef.org/media/media_96452.html.

Varoufakis, Yanis. *Adults in the Room: My battle with Europe's deep establishment*. New York: Random House, 2017.

Walker, R. B. J. *Inside/Outside: International relations as political theory*. Cambridge: Cambridge University Press, 1992.

Weber, Max. *Weber's Rationalism and Modern Society*. Translated by Tony Waters and Dagmar Waters. New York and Basingstoke: Palgrave Macmillan, 2015.

Weil, Patrick. *Qu'est-ce qu'un français?* Paris: Grasset, 2002.

Yeats, W. B. *Collected Poems*. London: Picador, 1990.

Manifestos and platforms

Early on, after the onset of the economic crisis, economists were already arguing that Europe's response wasn't right: see 'Manifesto of the Appalled Economists' at https://euroalter.com/document/manifesto-of-the-appalled-economist.

A good summary of civil society proposals to address the economic crisis can be found in the IsiGrowth report 'How can Europe change?': see www.isigrowth.eu/2016/10/26/how-can-europe-change/.

The Citizens Manifesto brings together proposals for European reform devised through a participatory process of 80 citizens' assemblies across Europe: see www.citizenspact.eu.

The Charter of Lampedusa brought together hundreds of NGOs and social movements to craft an alternative European migration policy: see https://euroalter.com/projects/charter-of-lampedusa.

For an inspiring example of migrants and artists jointly articulating a new global condition, see the Migrant Movement Manifesto at http://immigrant-movement.us/wordpress/migrant-manifesto/.

For an attempt at bottom-up transnational labour coordination, see the Transnational Strike Platform at www.transnational-strike. info/.

There have been several attempts to rejuvenate political alternatives at the transnational level. Among them, the pan-European movement DiEM25 was launched in early 2016 with a manifesto for change: see www.diem25.org.

For an attempt to bring together social movements and left-wing forces in Eastern Europe, see the Democratic Left 18 Manifesto at www.demleft.net.

For an overview of Europe's new municipalist movement, rich with links for further reading, see Beppe Caccia's introduction to Europe's New Municipalism at http://politicalcritique.org/world/2017/from-citizen-platforms-to-fearless-cities-europes-new-municipalism/.

Index

1930s 9, 73, 124
16+1 grouping 80

African National
    Congress 181, 190
Airbnb 195
Alibaba 114
Allende, Salvador 62
Alternative für
    Deutschland 27, 29
Amare Phrala 152
Amazon 95, 113, 114, 214
Amnesty 161, 175
Apple 106, 107, 113
Arab Spring 135
Arendt, Hannah 118
artificial intelligence 53
Asian Investment Bank 80
Asian Social Forum 177
austerity 27, 35, 101, 102

Bakunin, Mikhail 167, 173
Baobab experience 130
Barber, Benjamin 202
Barcelona en Comu 195
Basescu, Traian 151
Beckett, Samuel 210
Bellamy, Edward 11, 200

Belt and Road Initiative 80
Benario, Olga and Braun,
    Otto 168
Benavidez, Susana 93
Bentham, Jeremy 58, 138, 162
Berlin Wall 43, 63
Besant, Annie 98
Blair, Tony 43, 45, 63
Blockupy 101
Borges, Jorge Luis 47
Borissov, Boyko 151
Brecht, Bertold 142
Bretton Woods 73, 74, 76, 77,
    88, 175
Brexit 1, 2, 5, 6, 16, 27, 29, 40,
    44, 78, 146, 192
Britain 1, 90, 99
British Empire 72
Bundia, Devshi 91
Burke, Edmund 104
Burrows, Herbert 99
Bush, George W. 43

Cameron, David 150
Campaign for Nuclear
    Disarmament 175
capitalism 26, 27, 32, 48, 56,
    70, 74, 75, 140, 175, 180

CETA (Comprehensive Economic and Trade Agreement) 207
Charlie Hebdo 142
Charter of Lampedusa 131
China 24, 25, 60, 79, 80, 100, 113, 114, 180
Chinese Communist Party 24, 182
citizens 1, 2, 3, 4, 5, 9, 11, 12, 16, 17, 18, 20, 21, 33, 34, 38, 39, 41, 45, 48, 50, 51, 64, 66, 67, 68, 84, 90, 91, 99, 102, 103, 109, 110, 111, 113, 114, 116, 117, 123, 126, 130, 132, 133, 136, 137, 138, 139, 140, 141, 142, 143, 146, 147, 148, 151, 153, 155, 156, 157, 160, 161, 162, 164, 176, 177, 178, 179, 181, 182, 183, 184, 187, 189, 191, 194, 197, 198, 200, 202, 206, 208, 209, 210 211, 212, 213, 214
citizens assemblies 38
citizens manifesto 38
citizens of the world 3, 4, 138, 189, 210, 213
citizenship 3, 4, 6, 7, 12, 46, 48, 117, 124, 131, 136, 137, 138, 139, 140, 141, 142, 143, 144, 145, 146, 147, 148, 150, 151, 153, 154, 155, 156, 161, 168, 181, 200, 210, 214, 215
City Plaza Hotel Athens 129, 130

climate change 4, 196
Clinton, Bill 45, 63
Cloots, Anacharsis 138
Colau, Ada 68
Colorni, Eugenio 172
Committee of the Regions 202
Common European Asylum System 128
commons, common good 99, 100–101, 113–115, 195
Conservative Party 1, 2, 104
constituent assembly (Europe) 210–212
Constituent Assembly (French Revolution) 137, 162
Convention on the Reduction of Statelessness 142
Corbyn, Jeremy 71, 78
Council of Europe 140, 194

Declaration of the Rights of Man and of the Citizen 137, 162
Deliveroo 94, 95
democracy 8, 51, 23–27, 37, 39, 50, 56, 74, 66, 86, 103, 104, 111, 113, 114, 115, 116, 117, 135, 146, 147, 148, 156, 157, 173, 174, 182, 183, 186, 187, 189, 190, 195, 196, 199, 206, 209, 210, 212
demos 190
Depardieu, Gérard 145
Desai, Jayaben 91, 93, 115
Desire Foundation 152

detention centres 132, 133, 154

Dickens, Charles 98

digital economy 114

Diogenes the Cynic 161

Double Irish 106

Droste effect 185

Dublin agreement 154

Dutch Sandwich 106

eBay 114

Engels, Friedrich 83, 169

Enlightenment 55, 56

Erdogan, Recep Tayyip 127

Estrosi, Christian 122

euro 33, 45, 69, 85

Eurogroup 20, 34, 103

Europa 6–8, 188

European Alternatives 16, 17, 35, 36, 97, 99, 133, 149, 150, 152, 202, 207, 208, 214

European Central Bank 22, 101

European Charter of the Commons 100

European Citizens Initiative 38

European Commission 45, 85, 108, 128, 147, 155

European Commons Assembly 100–101, 113

European Constitution 13, 212

European Council 45, 109, 155, 207, 208

European Court of Justice 86, 135, 155

European Economic Community 63, 84

European elections 37–38, 208–211

European Federalist Movement 172

European Network on Debt and Development 105

European Parliament 36, 100, 108, 116, 172, 174, 203, 207, 208, 209, 210, 211

European People's Party (EPP) 37, 38

European Refugee Fund 128

European Semester 85

European Social Forum 177, 179

eurozone 43, 82, 86, 103, 112, 113, 187

EU–Turkey Agreement 127, 205

Facebook 113, 114, 173

Fanelli, Giuseppe 166

federation 84, 87, 90, 105, 166, 167, 174, 183, 209

Fico, Robert 146

financial transaction tax 112

First World War 9, 72, 124, 164, 169

Fiscal Compact 85, 207

Five Star Movement 40

Foodora 94

Ford, Henry 89

Fordism 60, 76

Foucault, Michel 147, 161, 183
France 13, 15, 27, 46, 48, 67, 98, 118, 121, 123, 124, 134, 138, 139, 142, 144, 145, 150, 151, 152, 155, 170
Fraser, Nancy 75
free markets 31, 57, 60, 65, 70, 73, 75, 84
free movement 48, 84, 86, 146, 189, 191, 206
French National Convention (French Revolution) 124, 138
French Revolution 8, 124, 137, 138, 139, 149, 160, 162
Friedman, Milton 62
Frontex 128

G7 175
G20 175
Galeano, Eduardo 7
Gandhi, Mahatma 164
Geneva Convention 120
Germany 28, 45, 47, 67, 90, 95, 96, 99, 101, 102, 124, 126, 127, 150, 168, 170, 172, 196
gig economy 28, 94–96, 115, 195
Giotto 185
Giustizia e Libertà 172
global justice movement 176, 177
globalisation 2, 5, 30, 43, 71, 72, 73, 77, 89, 115, 157, 173, 174, 175, 176, 177, 180, 186

Glorious Revolution 184
Godot 210
Google 90, 107, 113, 114
Gramsci, Antonio 13, 41–44
Great Depression 31, 66, 124
The Great Transformation 57
Greenpeace 175
Grillo, Beppe 40
Grunwick strike 91

Hanbury Hall 98
Havel, Vaclav 64, 160
Hayek, Friedrich 59, 84, 86, 87, 88, 90, 104
Herrou, Céderic 121, 122, 125, 205
Hirschmann, Ursula 170–172, 174
Hitler, Adolph 170, 171
Hollande, François 124, 142, 145
hostile environment 133

ideology 3, 56, 62, 64, 84, 87, 88, 90, 174, 179, 193
Ikea 108
Il Gattopardo 50
Il Postino 109–110
illiberal democracy 70, 180
IMF 22, 76, 80, 175
Independent Workers Union of Great Britain 94
Indian National Congress 98, 181, 190
Industrial Revolution 8

Index

Industrial Workers of the World 94

Inicjatywa Pracownicza 96

interdependency 79, 111, 157, 185, 193, 199

international settlements and disputes system (ISDS) 116

International Workingmen's Association 165, 166, 167

interregnum 13, 41

intersectionality 191

Iraq War 43

Italy 15, 36, 37, 40, 43, 44, 67, 94, 99, 100, 118, 121, 124, 128, 133, 165

Jaurès, Jean 164

JD.com 114

Johnson and Johnson 106–107

Justice for Cleaners 94

Kafka, Franz 30, 125

Kant, Immanuel 160

Kautsky, Karl 169

Kazynski, Jaroslaw 38

Klaus, Vaclav 64

Kuron, Jacek 159

Kurz, Sebastian 47

Labour Party 2, 26, 93

laissez-faire 57, 58, 61, 65, 72

Le Pen, Marine 27, 49

Lenin, Vladimir 170

liberalism 25, 57, 58, 65, 72

Lisbon Treaty 207

lobbyist 35

London Festival of Europe 15, 99

London Fight Club 14

London Trades Council 98

Looking Backwards 11

Machiavelli, Niccolò 204

Mannon, Pierre-Alain 121, 122, 125, 146, 147, 205

Mao Zedong 168

Marx, Eleanor 99

Marx, Karl 83, 165, 167, 169, 173

Match Girls 98

Mauss, Marcel 164

May, Theresa 1, 2, 3, 6, 140, 141, 213

Mazzini, Giuseppe 163, 165, 166, 167, 173

Médecins Du Monde 147, 161, 175

media pluralism 37–39

Merkel, Angela 34, 45, 126, 127, 150

Microsoft 113

Migreurop 133, 134

Mirabeau, Francois 162

de Miranda, Francisco 162

Moebius strip 189

Monnet, Jean 105

Morris, William 10, 55, 90, 200

multi-speed Europe 39

Napoleon 55

nation 2, 6, 13, 54, 57, 71, 78, 79, 82, 83, 87, 102, 103, 104, 106, 108, 110, 112, 117, 127, 129, 137, 138, 139, 140, 141, 148, 162, 163, 164, 165, 167, 168, 169, 173, 182, 183, 184, 186, 187, 188, 195, 197, 202, 206, 209, 214

nationalisation 11, 82, 90

nationalism 2, 3, 48, 73, 81, 88, 89, 90, 93, 103, 104, 105, 114, 117, 146, 164, 174, 192, 196

nationality 55, 87, 90, 109, 145, 147, 148, 156, 173, 193

neoliberalism 6, 32, 59, 61, 62, 63, 64, 66, 71, 73, 76, 77, 81, 83, 84, 89, 102, 103, 104, 105, 110, 115, 117, 173, 174, 175, 180, 182, 188, 191, 192, 200, 209

Neruda, Pablo 109

New Deal 31, 61, 63, 73

New Labour 63

News from Nowhere 10–11

nostalgia 8–9, 12, 74, 75

Obama, Barack 28, 31, 32

Odysseus 9, 159, 160

Opium Wars 72

Orban, Viktor 38, 44, 69

Owen, Robert 65

PAH (Platform for People affected by Mortgages) 67–68

Paine, Thomas 138

panopticon 58

parliament of mayors 202

Pata Rat 152

Pestes, Luis Carlos 168

Pfizer 106

Pinochet, Augusto 62

Podemos 21, 39, 195

Poe, Edgar Allen 55

Poland 95, 96, 180

Polanyi, Karl 57, 64, 66, 74, 186

populism 66

Portugal 108

precarity 10, 49

Priestley, Joseph 138

quantitative easing 32

Rau, Milo 202

Rebel Roo 94

Reding, Viviane 150

Referendum 13, 22, 99

Regan, Ronald 62

Renren 114

returns directive 133

Robespierre 162

Rojava 187

Roma 147, 148, 150, 151, 152, 155

Romania 28, 100, 135, 149, 151, 192

Roosevelt, Franklin D. 68

Rosselli, Carlo 159

Rossi, Ernesto 172

Russian Revolution 47

Index

Sanders, Bernie 78

Sarkozy, Nicolas 43, 150

Schauble, Wolfgang 103

Second World War 73, 75, 84, 164, 171

Shakespeare, William 27, 185

Silicon Valley 113–114

Simon, Herbert 53

social movements 18, 21, 74, 131, 194, 211

socialism in one country 83, 170, 173

Solidarność 96

sovereignty 6, 82, 138, 147–149, 163

Spain 21, 39, 43, 66, 67, 95, 144, 167, 186, 195

Spinelli, Altiero 172, 174, 211

Stalin, Joseph 170, 173

Stigliz, Joseph 59

Stockholm Program 133

Strache 46

Suez Crisis 75

Sun Yat-sen 164

Syntagma Square 21

Syriza 20, 21, 22, 23, 34, 46, 103

take back control 5–6, 41, 81, 114, 146, 186

Taoism 60

tax havens 105, 111

Teatro Valle Occupato 100

Temporary Protection Directive 128

Tencents 114

Terre Des Hommes 161

Thatcher, Margaret 63, 93

Third Way 62

Titus Livius (Livy) 204

Trade Union Congress 93

Transeuropa Festival 99, 101

Transition period (Eastern Europe) 63

Transnational Social Strike Platform 95

Trans-Pacific trade agreement 89

Treaty of Rome 84

trentes glorieuses 74

Troika 22, 34

Trotsky, Leon 170, 173

Trump, Donald 27, 29, 40, 44, 78, 89, 110, 142, 192

TTIP 207

Tusk, Donald 23, 42

Twitter 114

Uber 28, 94

UK 2, 26, 28, 91, 92, 93, 94, 142, 146, 203, 213

UK Home Office 141

Union of Women's Match Makers 99

United Nations 126, 140, 183, 194

United Voices of the World 94

Universal Declaration of Human Rights 142

utopia 7, 8, 10, 11, 12, 13, 17, 108, 189, 200, 201, 213, 214

Ventotene Manifesto 172, 174
Verdi (trade union) 95, 96
Viking and Laval
    judgements 86
Vlora cargo ship 128

Washington, George 138
Weber, Max 12
Weibo 114
Wilson, Woodrow 164
World Bank 76, 175
World Economic Forum 175
World Social Forum 176–179

World Trade Organisation
    (WTO) 175–176
worldview 174–175, 191

Xi Jinping 79, 180

Yahoo 107
Yeats, W.B. 44
young people 4–5, 10, 28–29,
    32, 49

Zeus 6
zombies 42

ZED

Zed is a platform for marginalised voices across the globe.

It is the world's largest publishing collective and a world leading example of alternative, non-hierarchical business practice.

It has no CEO, no MD and no bosses and is owned and managed by its workers who are all on equal pay.

It makes its content available in as many languages as possible.

It publishes content critical of oppressive power structures and regimes.

It publishes content that changes its readers' thinking.

It publishes content that other publishers won't and that the establishment finds threatening.

It has been subject to repeated acts of censorship by states and corporations.

It fights all forms of censorship.

It is financially and ideologically independent of any party, corporation, state or individual.

Its books are shared all over the world.

www.zedbooks.net
@ZedBooks